SINGLE

SINGLE
The Woman's View

Marilyn McGinnis

FLEMING H. REVELL COMPANY
Old Tappan, New Jersey

Library of Congress Cataloging in Publication Data

McGinnis, Marilyn.
    Single; the woman's view.

    1. Single women—Conduct of life. 2. Single
women—Religious life. I. Title.
BJ1610.M29   248'.4   74-9837
ISBN 0-8007-0678-1

TO my parents
who taught me how to be a Christian woman
and
TO my husband
who's glad I am one

Contents

Preface

When I turned thirty my mother declared that life for me was about to change. She had given me thirty years to find a husband, she said, and I hadn't succeeded. So she was taking over with definite plans to remedy the situation.

Her first three candidates for the esteemed position of son-in-law (complete with newspaper clippings and photos for two of them) were as follows:

1. Barry Goldwater, Jr. (because my father likes his father). He was still a bachelor then.
2. A pharmacist in Oskaloosa, Iowa (for health reasons she thought it would be economically advantageous to have a pharmacist in the family). She found his picture in a discarded newspaper when she and my father were depositing trash at the local dump.
3. An ex-con living in Phoenix who was supposedly going straight. My mother believes in giving a person a second chance. But there was some question about whether or not his business was legitimate. At the time there was a possibility he would be asked to leave Phoenix.

My father said if I didn't marry one of the men mother picked out he was going to give me away—not in marriage—for adoption!

Parental opinion to the contrary, being single isn't all bad. As a matter of fact, it has some distinct advantages that can never be

9

found in marriage. Throughout my single years I saw (and still see) single women who are leading happy, productive lives. Some marry. Some don't. Their lives are a happy example of the plan God has for every single person's life. I also see many single women floundering at age thirty and thirty-five with bitterness, insecurities, resentment, and other problems that should have been resolved at twenty-five. What makes the difference?

The purpose of this book is to help you discover the happiness and fulfillment God has for you during your single years. It's there for the taking. Don't let it get away!

I am deeply grateful for Jan Brown, Arlene Commings, and Peggy Miller, who evaluated the manuscript and offered valuable suggestions, and for my husband, George, whose masculine viewpoint helped me sharpen my thinking.

I am also grateful to the many single Christian women across the country, from California to Boston, who shared their views on the single life via a questionnaire. Many of their comments confirmed my own views about the single life. Others gave me new food for thought. You'll find many of their thoughts and ideas woven throughout the pages of this book.

The single women mentioned in this book are real people. Only the names and a few of the facts have been changed to prevent embarrassment.

SINGLE

. . . firmly grasp what you know to
be the will of the Lord.

Ephesians 5:17 PHILLIPS

1

Why Isn't a Nice Girl
Like You Married?

The Single Choice

"Why isn't a nice girl like you married?"

How many times have people said that to you? Bet you nickles to knee socks you lost count long ago.

It starts right after you graduate from college. (Everybody *else* got married before they graduated.) You come bounding home some weekend bubbling with news about your first job. And what happens? Some well-meaning neighbor lady or an ancient aunt puts a damper on everything.

"But, my dear," she wails, loud enough for half the neighborhood to hear, "why isn't a nice girl like you married?"

For the next few years that question is always popping up. And every woman who asks you (how come it's always women?) is naively sure she's the only person who has ever asked you that question—or for that matter, the only person who is *really* concerned about your single state.

The closer you get to thirty, the less people are apt to ask. By this time they're thoroughly convinced there must be something dreadfully wrong with you—like beriberi or the tsetse fly. And, for the sake of your family, at least, who must bear the awful stigma, they dare not ask. (If they do ask, you might be tempted to reply, "I am," and leave them guessing, or "I have been—five times" and leave them stretched out in a faint.)

13

But sooner or later somebody will ask it again. "Why isn't a nice girl like you married?"

Well, why aren't you?

Honestly, now. Why aren't you married? There must be a reason.

Is it because nobody ever asked you? I doubt that. Think back into the past and you're likely to come up with *somebody* who at least hinted at marriage. It may have been that boy with buck teeth you hated in the fourth grade. But it was somebody.

Is it because you're so ugly nobody will look at you? I doubt that, too. It does have possibilities, though. But only if you're ugly on the inside, not the outside.

Is it because you have such a horrible personality people flee from you like you have the proverbial plague? I doubt that, too. The real you down underneath is a delightful person. Maybe you have trouble sometimes letting the real you show. But I still doubt that's the real reason why you aren't married.

Well, then, if it isn't because no one ever asked you, or you're too ugly, or have a horrible personality, what *is* the reason?

Almost without exception, a single woman (who has never been married) is single *by choice*.

"Not *me!*" I can hear you wailing already. "If you think for one minute I want to be single you've got another think coming. I'd like nothing better than to trade my single bed in for a double."

Okay, so relax. Did I say you were single because you don't *want* to be married? No. There are many reasons why women (and men, too, for that matter) choose to be single. Some are conscious reasons. Some are subconscious. Let's look at a few of them.

Career Today—To Stay

Some girls choose not to marry, or to delay marriage, in order to pursue a career. These girls are usually intelligent, creative, dedicated (an overworked term, I'll admit), and thoroughly enjoy the working world. They often take graduate work after college and successfully climb the ladder in their chosen field.

Some of these women are really quite content being single. One woman who works with girls in a religious organization faced the decision of whether God really wanted her to remain single in her work. She asked God that, if He could use her best as a single woman, He would take away the desire for a husband and family. And God did just that. This enabled her to serve God without the tensions of a strong desire for marriage.

Missionary women fall into the career category, too, although not all of them are against the idea of marriage. A single woman who chooses to serve in a remote corner of the world faces the possibility that there may be no single Christian men where she serves. In effect she is choosing to be single. Certainly God often intervenes and brings the right single man her way. Missionary biographies are full of such delightful stories. But if you choose missionary service you had better face the possibility of remaining single and evaluate yourself accordingly. Can you or can you not cope with life without a man?

Alice in Happily-Ever-After Land

Remember the Grace Livingston Hill novels when you were a kid? I grew up on them. I read them by the bushel basketful and dreamed those childish romantic dreams of adolescence. Every romance in every book was perfect. He was the gallant hero. She was the shy and beautiful maiden. Problems were minor or nonexistent, or so enchantingly solved that they only added to the storybook quality of the romance. The couple always lived happily ever after.

Unfortunately, some girls grow up with just that kind of an unrealistic approach toward men and marriage. They're looking for the ideal man, the gallant hero of their childhood, the knight in shining armor to literally sweep them off their feet. (Pity the woman who marries with this attitude. She finds out in a hurry that perfect husbands and perfect marriages do not exist.) No man quite measures up. Like the missionary I once knew who used to jokingly tell her friends she was keeping a nice long list of the qualities she wanted in a husband. After quite a few years of list keeping, her friends finally counseled her, "For pity's sake,

Madge, at your age throw away the list!" She finally married when she was well past forty.

I hate to prick your bubble, but if you're looking for the perfect husband you are, in effect, choosing to be single. You'd *better* be choosing to be single. Heaven help the man who marries you! Perfect men don't exist. Perfect women don't exist either. Think about that. And if that doesn't move you to face reality, maybe this will. I understand Grace Livingston Hill had a poor marriage. Her first marriage was fine, but when husband number one died she remarried. Her second marriage was a mistake. She and husband number two were separated for many years.

The I-Hate-Men Syndrome

The opposite of "idealistic Alice" is the female with the I-hate-men attitude. You know the kind. You can spot them a mile away.

Your father was a brute and mistreated your mother so all men are brutes.

One man courted you—and dumped you. Now you'll never trust another man as long as you live.

Your best girl friend stole your boyfriend and now most of your friends are married. Every time you look at any of them you get sick with jealousy. Why should they have it so good when you have it so bad?

Poor you. Really have it bad, don't you? Before you know it resentment piles upon bitterness with a little jealousy thrown in for good measure. You retreat into your own self-centered world of self-pity, and even your mother can hardly stand to be around you.

No wonder nobody's asked you out for an age. No guy wants to date a girl who's a drag. Or a girl who makes him feel like he never should have happened. If you're harboring a crummy attitude toward men—or toward yourself—don't expect men to beat a path to your third floor walk-up. Consciously or unconsciously you are choosing to be single—if you don't make an effort to change.

Parental Priorities

Joan was the youngest child in her family — one of those later-in-life babies who grow up almost like an only child. By the time she finished high school her parents were elderly and her sisters had long since left home to make a life of their own. Somebody had to look after her parents and Joan got the job by default. She dutifully cared for them and looked after their home. After her father died she finally got married at the age of twenty-eight.

Susan's little sister was very small when their mother died. Their father was an alcoholic and Susan and her older sister felt it was their responsibility to raise their baby sister. Susan got a job to help support the family. Her older sister stayed home to look after the family. Susan took her little sister to church regularly and encouraged her in the Christian life. A year or two after her sister, now grown, married one of the boys from the church, Susan died of a serious heart condition. She was thirty-six.

Some girls delay marriage plans — or abandon them altogether — in order to care for their parents, or to raise younger brothers and sisters. On the surface this looks like a commendable choice. And in many instances it is. But parental priorities can also be a cover-up for a girl who is emotionally immature and unable to cope with the idea of a normal date life and possible marriage.

If the need is genuine the choice is commendable. In some instances where a parent is an invalid and there is no other relative to care for him or her, a daughter's unselfish choice to take care of her parent is commendable. In Susan's case where the baby sister would have been raised by an alcoholic father, her choice was a wise one.

But what about the girl who uses parental priorities as an escape from emotional maturity? She is actually tied to her parents and unable to break away from them. For example, every time you plan a weekend trip to the mountains, your mother gets deathly ill and you have to cancel your plans. Or whenever a man asks you for a date, you back off and tell him you can't leave your ailing mother. The ties that bind a parent and child are sometimes never severed. The child remains an emotional cripple all of his or her life.

In other situations, the single daughter is often *expected* to care for her aging parents, especially if the rest of her brothers and sisters are married. This is unfair. But it happens all the time. The married brothers and sisters don't want to be bothered and the easiest thing is to "let Joan do it." And Joan, not realizing the trap into which she is falling, shoulders the burden alone.

If you are caring for one or both of your parents, ask yourself these questions:

Why am I caring for my parents? Could any other member of my family share this responsibility?

How many close friends do I have?

Do I ever attend social events with my friends without my parents going along?

Is my parent's illness genuine? Or is he or she holding a real or imagined illness over my head to keep me at home?

If my parents don't really need me, how would I feel about leaving home and starting a life of my own? Am I using my parents as a crutch to avoid having to go it alone?

Sometimes it's difficult to evaluate correctly a situation when you are in the middle of it. If you have trouble answering any of these questions, ask your close friends or your family doctor what they think. Tell them you want honest answers.

I'll Wait, Thanks

There are some girls, and I hope you're one of them, who aren't looking for just any old guy who comes along. They're looking for the *right* man. Not some knight in shining armor from the land of make-believe. A real man who is the right man—the man who is God's choice for that girl's life. And good things don't just happen. They take time. Some girls have to wait a long time for the right man. But when they find him, they discover that the wait was more than worth it.

The next time you get mad at the world and start blaming God because you aren't married, just remember—you've *chosen* to be single. Any girl who is willing to lower her standards can get married if she wants to.

Let's assume, then, that you're single by choice for one reason or another. And having chosen to be single—permanently or temporarily—you'd like to make the most of your single years. The rest of this book is devoted to helping you do just that.

2

If the WITCHes Don't Get You, Pussycats Will

The Search for the Real You

Being a woman in today's world is rather confusing business. If you've done any reading lately on the subject of femininity you may have concluded that a lot of women don't really know who they are.

The first things you learned about being a woman you probably learned from your mother, your older sister, your grandmother, and your high-school home economics teacher, in that order. From the time you were old enough to hold things in your two chubby hands, you latched onto a doll. And for the next ten or twelve years you spent hours role playing what it's like to be a wife and mother. You cooked, washed dishes, cleaned, sewed clothes for your dolly, and regally commanded the bewildered neighbor boy to stop tracking in dirt on your nice clean playroom floor. Being a woman meant homework, housework, being submissive to one's husband, and raising a batch of kiddies. That was all any woman needed.

Then along came Betty Friedan and blew everything you'd ever learned. Woman is unfulfilled, she wailed. The modern wife is trapped in her home. She is a victim of every traveling salesman because she's bored, bored, bored. "Emancipate womankind!" was her battle cry. Let women get out and work in the world so they can discover their "true identity."

So they got out and went to work. Millions of them. The labor force is crawling with women. Married ones. Single ones. And in-betweeners. At last womankind was about to find her "true identity."

But a funny thing happened on the way to the office. A certain segment of women discovered that they didn't have any "true identity" in the working world, either. Or so they thought. The world is against us, they cried. Especially the world of men. We're discriminated against. Our salaries are too low. We want equal rights with men. The wife who was trapped in her home is now trapped at the switchboard. The unhappy house frau who was a victim of the traveling salesman is now a victim of the executive vice-president. Hurling typewriters and steno pads to the wind, the Women's Liberation Movement was born. Women declared war.

First we've got unhappy housewives. Now we've got unhappy working women. Both unable to find their "true identity."

So what is identity, anyway? Is it *where* you are? Or *what* you're doing? Does "equality with men" help you find out who you are? Or is identity the *real you* down inside—no matter *what* you may be doing?

Okay, so who are you? Come on now, think. Who are you really? Lots of single girls have an identity problem which even Women's Lib hasn't been able to solve. This identity problem keeps them from making friends, getting ahead in their jobs, and from being attractive to the right kind of men.

So let's take a look at you. Get yourself a piece of paper and write down everything you know about yourself—your physical, mental, emotional, social, and spiritual qualities, and anything else that comes to mind. Ask God to help you evaluate yourself *as you are.* Be honest, but don't be hard on yourself. When in doubt, give yourself the benefit of the doubt. You're probably harder on yourself than anyone else would be. Your list should look something like this:

Here's a Picture of Me

Physical	Mental	Emotional	Social	Spiritual
Good posture	Average IQ	Sometimes have trouble controlling my temper	Enjoy parties	Feel like God is far away at times and not interested in me
Ten pounds overweight	Hate to read		Hate to be home alone	
Good teeth	Enjoy discussing new ideas		Have difficulty starting conversations	Enjoy reading the Bible but prayer is difficult
Nice smile				

Now get another piece of paper. Mark two columns on the paper and label one "Assets" and the other "Liabilities." Place each item listed on the first sheet in the appropriate column.

Assets	Liabilities
Good posture	Ten pounds overweight
Average IQ	Hate to read
Enjoy discussing new ideas	Sometimes have trouble controlling my temper
Enjoy parties	Hate to be home alone
Enjoy reading the Bible	Have difficulty starting conversations
Good teeth	Feel like God is far away at times and not interested in me
Nice smile	Prayer is difficult

Unless you're a hopeless masochist, you probably have several items listed in the "Assets" column. These are your strong points and there are probably more you haven't thought of.

Is your weight about right for your height (give or take a couple of hot fudge sundaes)? Good. Keep it that way.

Do you like to read? Are you interested in current events?

Great. That's one of the first steps toward being an interesting conversationalist.

Can you keep your cool when everyone else in the office is mad at the boss? Excellent. You probably have good self-control.

Are you interested in other people? Do you enjoy making new friends? You score again. Nothing charms a person (including men) quite so much as feeling that someone is genuinely interested in him.

Are you trying to live out your Christian faith as best you can with God's help? If so, then you're in touch with the One in whom we find our true identity—Jesus Christ.

Now take a look at the "Liabilities" column.

Got middle-age spread already and you're barely twenty-five? Get rid of that excess flab. All the girdles in the world won't conceal it. Or maybe you're the opposite kind, always starving yourself silly so you can wear your roommate's size three. Result? An anemic size three who ought to be a size ten. A pale, hollow-eyed waif isn't going to attract a guy any more than a flabby Flo. Good health is valuable. It means color in the cheeks, a sparkle in the eye, and fewer doctor bills.

How about your mental qualities? When was the last time you read a book, or an editorial in the newspaper, or went to a "think" movie? Put nothing into your brain and you can be sure nothing will come out. There you are at a party just dying to talk to a certain good-looking guy, but you're tongue-tied. Had you at least read the newspaper before you came you might try this for an opener, "I believe I overhead you say you are in the insurance business. I read an article in the paper the other day that said insurance rates are being adjusted because of new zoning regulations. How does that affect your work?"

What's your emotional temperature? Are you easily offended? Always mad at somebody? Some people spend enormous amounts of energy unconsciously collecting injustices. They continually complain of being snubbed, rebuffed, or mistreated— most of which is entirely in their own heads. The result? A prickly pear that nobody much wants to be around. Or are you just the opposite—always bending over backward to please people so that the real you gets lost behind a mask of super polite do-goodishness?

Where do you fit on the social scale? Are you the life of the party, a shy little wallflower, or somewhere in between? Do you make an effort to get out and meet people, or stay at home moping because you don't have any friends?

How's your spiritual life? When was the last time you read the Bible (really read it, not just a verse or two at bedtime to salve your conscience)? Or told God exactly how you feel about something with no holds barred? Or heard Him speak to you? As a Christian, what are the gifts God is developing in you? What are you doing to tell others about the wonderful love God has shown to you? Or have you never experienced that wonderful love?

Evaluating your assets and liabilities is going to take time. You can't do it on a ten-minute coffee break. It may take a week, a month or a year. The important thing is to be honest with yourself. Ask God to reveal additional assets and liabilities you may have missed. Perhaps a close friend can be of help. But here let me offer a word of caution. Don't ask a friend for an honest evaluation unless you are prepared to accept it—good, bad, or indifferent. Your minister or a Christian counselor might be a more objective source of help.

Once you have evaluated yourself as objectively as possible, the next step is to note those areas where definite change is necessary. Keep the list short. If you make it too long you'll be discouraged before you start. List only four or five things that you honestly feel are keeping you from being the kind of person you want to be and the kind of person God wants you to be.

Pray about the changes that need to be made. Not a casual, "Oh, God, please help me to change" type of prayer. But a specific prayer for specific changes. ". . . let God transform you inwardly by a complete change of your mind. Then you will be able to know the will of God—what is good, and is pleasing to him, and is perfect" (Romans 12:2 TEV). If you tend to become discouraged easily, remember that no problem is too great for

God to solve. "Let your hope keep you joyful, be patient in your troubles, and pray at all times" (Romans 12:12 TEV).

Some changes will be obvious. Are you thirty pounds overweight? Go on a diet—a sensible diet, recommended by your doctor, that won't leave you limp and listless. Are you a hostile person who is constantly criticizing others? Swallow your pride and visit a competent Christian counselor. Once you discover what makes you so hostile, half the battle is solved. But only half. The rest depends upon you. Not until you decide with God's help to *stop* criticizing people and *start* loving them will any real progress be made. God's commandment that we "love one another" must not be taken lightly.

How about your appearance? Are you the plainest of plain Janes? Is your hair a pile of straw, your clothes something less than chic? There's help available all around you. What woman do you know whose hair always looks shiny and beautiful? Ask her how she takes care of her hair and where she has it done. She will be flattered by the compliment and eager to help you. If you need help choosing the right clothes for your figure and wearing them properly, why not sign up for a charm-school course? You'll learn what styles are best for you, how to walk and talk properly, and how to put your best foot forward. If you belong to a single-adult group, you might suggest that the girls meet together occasionally and invite a beautician, model, or other appropriate person to discuss and help you with your appearance.

The goal of every Christian woman, whether married or single, should be to attract people to Jesus Christ. This does not mean you must be a raving beauty or a personality queen. It does mean you must let Jesus Christ work through you to develop your personality—the personality He gave you. There is no room in His plan for carbon copies. He made you unique and He wants you to serve Him in the "uniquely you" way He intended.

Sometimes our personalities become hidden behind a mask of fear, hostility, sin, and a host of other cover-ups. So hidden, in fact, that we don't really know who we are—and neither does anybody else. A guilty conscience can drive you into a way of life that hardly resembles the person God wants you to be. But once the chains of guilt are broken and you are forgiven by God, a whole new world will open up.

Jesus Christ has promised to set us free. With His help, "Let us rid ourselves, then, of everything that gets in the way, and the sin which holds on to us so tightly, and let us run with determination the race that lies before us. Let us keep our eyes fixed on Jesus . . ." (Hebrews 12:1, 2 TEV).

O wad some Power the giftie gie us
To see oursels as ithers see us!
It wad frae monie a blunder free us,
An' foolish notion.

ROBERT BURNS

3

Are You Fun to Know?

You and Your Personality

She was being interviewed for a secretarial position in our office and the interview was going very badly. The conversation went something like this.

THE BOSS   Do you know how to type?

SHE   Not very well.

BOSS   Do you take shorthand?

SHE   No.

BOSS   Have you had any experience working in an office?

SHE   Well, not really. I really haven't done much of anything like this.

She didn't know how to do anything and her ability to handle an interview was batting zero. In a desperate attempt to keep the interview from utterly collapsing, my boss, always the Christian gentleman, said graciously, "Well, at least you have a pleasant personality."

At which point the girl gushed uncontrollably, "Oh, *do I?*"

What is personality, anyway? That illusive entity that draws us to some people and away from others. Webster refers to it as "identity," "distinctive personal character," "individuality," "magnetic personal quality," "the totality of an individual's characteristics." If the totality of those characteristics is basically positive, we say a person has a "wonderful personality." If the

characteristics are negative, we say he has a "lousy personality."
We're attracted to one person and repelled by another, largely
on the basis of personality.

There is no stereotype for the ideal personality, except for the
fact that a pleasant personality abounds with positive characteristics. How often do you find yourself envying the person who is
the life of the party, or the girl who seems to attract every man
she meets? All of us want to be attractive to others. But some
of us have trouble recognizing the qualities we need in order to
be attractive.

The first step toward developing a pleasant personality is to
realize that God *wants* you to be attractive to others. There is
nothing spiritual about repelling people. "The non-Christian is
not attracted to Jesus nor to you by the fact that you are 'different,'" suggests Rosalind Rinker in her book *You Can Witness
With Confidence*. Neither is another Christian. Jesus Christ was
the most attractive person who ever lived. And if He lives inside
of you then you can't help but be attractive, also. Granted there
were moments when people turned away from Him. But that was
because He spoke the truth and some people didn't want to hear
it.

As we discussed in chapter 2, you are a unique individual. The
personality God has given you, or the one He has waiting for you
if you've had trouble finding out who you are, is for you alone.
There are no carbon copies in God's creation. He wants you to be
you, not a miniature somebody else. He has created just the
personality that He wants you to have—the personality that will
make you a complete person, useful to Him, and attractive to
others. Because of this, you needn't spend your time trying to be
like somebody else. It just won't work. God wants you to be you.

What qualities make a person attractive to other people?

Individuality

Think of a single woman whose personality particularly
appeals to you. What is she like? What qualities make her attractive to other people? While you're thinking, let me share a
couple of my friends with you.

First there's Penny, a divorcée in her thirties. Anyone who's gone through a divorce (particularly a Christian) has suffered. And some women let the whole world know how tough life's been on them. Not Penny. She is bubbly and vivacious. Her life is filled with creative activities—camping, traveling, even a trip down the Colorado on a raft—and service to others—working with drug addicts, taking troubled teen-agers into her home from time to time. Her sense of humor never fades. She can tell you exactly what she thinks about something and you'd have to work overtime to resent her. Because she speaks with malice toward none—and with humor.

My other friend is Mary. Almost seventy. Never married, though she had plenty of chances when she was young. While Penny is bubbly and outgoing, Mary is quiet and reserved. Not too reserved, however. There is a warmth about her that envelops you. Her life is committed to serving Christ and His love is evident in everything she does. An experienced tour guide, she frequently takes groups to the Middle East. On one such trip I watched her, always the lady, suddenly burst into tears when unexpected trouble developed. My first reaction was surprise that she would cry in front of her tour members. But then I realized that because of who she is, it was really okay for her to cry. That brief burst of tears was just another evidence of her sweet, caring spirit. She wanted the best possible tour for us and we respected her for it.

Penny and Mary. Two completely different personalities. Both serving Christ in their own unique ways. Both completely honest about who they are. Not trying to be anyone else except themselves. Therein lies their charm.

Honesty

That brings us to the quality of honesty. A woman who is truly honest with herself and others is attractive. She can't help but be, because honesty is an attractive quality. Sin and deception may have their attractive moments. But in the long haul, truth will out, and man is attracted to truth.

To be anything else but honest is to cheat yourself out of the very best that God has for you. "O, what a tangled web we weave, When first we practise to deceive!" wrote Sir Walter Scott. The writer of Ecclesiastes puts it this way: "This alone I have found, that God, when he made man, made him straightforward, but man invents endless subtleties of his own." He prefaces this remark with the unhappy observation that, "after searching long without success: I have found one man in a thousand worth the name, but I have not found one woman among them all" (Ecclesiastes 7:29, 28 NEB).

Is it possible that women are even more prone to deception than men?

The ultimate source of truth, of course, is Jesus Christ. When you come face-to-face with Him, it's impossible to be deceptive. He made you and He knows exactly what goes on inside you. There isn't anything you can hide from Him. So why try? The important thing is that He knows you just exactly as you are — and accepts you. He doesn't accept the sin in your life, but neither does He reject *you* because of it. Instead He promises to forgive — and forget — when you come to Him in repentance.

Knowing that God accepts you as you are is an important step toward becoming a truly honest person. Unfortunately, however, other people are not always as accepting of us as God is. Some people learn early in life that honesty is not always rewarded. A friend told me one day how, as a child, she did something her father did not approve of. When he asked if she had done it, she lied and said no. "If you tell me the truth," he said, "I won't whip you." So she told him the truth and, as I recall, her confession was followed by a sound whipping. At that point she could easily have decided that honesty did not pay. Perhaps unconsciously she did.

The current generation of young people lays great stress on honesty. They're tired of the hypocrisy of their parents, they say. They want everyone to be honest and open. The whole sensitivity-training movement was born for just that reason — to help people pull off their masks and just be themselves.

True honesty, however, must be coupled with love. If your

roommate asks you what you think of her new dress and you bluntly tell her, "It's the ugliest thing I've ever seen," your honesty is not coupled with love. But to tell her you like it when it looks like a Goodwill reject is not being honest, either. If it's simply a matter of taste—she likes mod prints and your prefer Victorian ruffles—maybe it is the right dress for her. If, however, it is truly unflattering to her figure, you can tactfully suggest some alterations or even returning it.

Unselfishness

The single woman whose primary interest in life is helping others has little time to worry about being single. And her love and concern for others make her among the most attractive of women. A man notices a woman who is continually looking for ways to help others.

Now don't confuse the "helper" with the "people-pleaser." The helper is motivated by love. The people-pleaser is motivated by a super self-centered desire for acceptance. She'll do anything for anybody if it means gaining their approval. The helper, however, is motivated by an unselfish desire to share the love of Christ with others.

What are you doing for others? Right now. Today. If you are employed by a service-oriented organization, what are you doing for others in addition to that? By virtue of the fact that you are a human being of reasonable intelligence, not to mention the fact that you are a Christian, you have a God-given responsibility to others. Look around you. Everywhere you look there are people who need your help. Children who need tutoring, sick people who need food prepared or errands run, a Sunday-school class to be taught. It's even possible now for single people to adopt a child.

"Often God allows these relationships developed out of unselfish giving to become husband and/or children to a single woman," suggests a single friend, "if you are willing to really look at the role they end up playing or filling in your life." Get out of your own little world and give of yourself to other people.

A *Quiet Spirit*

For even the most outgoing personality, there is a time when the ability to simply remain quiet is an asset. Some people are quiet by nature. Others must develop it. Nothing will destroy your attractiveness so much as a mouth that never shuts off.

I have a couple of friends who never require a question ("How are you?" "What's up?") to get a conversation started. All I have to do is walk into their presence and they immediately begin telling me everything I ever wanted to know about anything and a whole lot more that I never did care to know. Solomon discovered that it was "Better to live in a corner of the house-top than have a nagging wife and a brawling household" (Proverbs 25:24 NEB). With a thousand wives and concubines he undoubtedly wrote from experience!

Coupled with a quiet spirit is the ability to listen. Remaining silent when there are a million things you'd like to say gives the other person a chance to share his thoughts which are every bit as important to him as yours are to you. When you care enough to remain silent and let *him* talk you show that you really do care.

A quiet spirit also prevents arguments, which usually arise when one or both parties are upset about something. It takes two people to make an argument. So if one party remains calm and quiet, it's impossible for the other person to argue alone. When everybody has cooled down, then you can discuss the issue rather than argue about it.

For another thing, I've discovered that many (most, if I'm really honest) of the things I'd like to say aren't really worth saying anyway. Letting the other person share his problem or his thoughts, rather than imposing mine upon him, usually accomplishes much more in the long run. It frees him to arrive at his own solutions. And when I sit back and quietly wait, I see God work things out in ways I never would have thought of or dreamed possible.

There is a time to speak. There are many more times when

one should simply remain silent. A quiet spirit is restful. A chatterbox drives a man bananas.

A Sense of Humor

I've just recovered from a week of depression. The doctor says it's because our first child is due in a couple of weeks and I'm very anxious to have the baby. Normally I don't have trouble with depression. But nearly every night last week found me in tears — with a different "problem" every night. I never knew I had so many problems!

At dinner one night I was again on the verge of puddling up when my husband came up with some witty remark that made me laugh. The more I laughed the harder it was to cry until I finally abandoned the idea altogether. His sense of humor is probably the one thing that helps him endure the wacky moods of a pregnant woman.

When was the last time you had a good laugh? Or made somebody else laugh? If you haven't laughed today over something, you're probably taking life entirely too seriously. Granted, life is serious, but all seriousness and no humor will send you to the funny farm. Ask God to give you the humility to see the humor in your own mistakes. When something goes wrong, look for the humorous side. It can't be *all* bad. Crack a joke. Have a good laugh. And the problem will be much easier to overcome.

Sunny-Side Up

In your list of qualities you most admire in a single woman, no doubt you included cheerfulness. We are irresistibly drawn to people who look on the bright side of things.

"It's so good to have Jerry on a committee," a church member said to our minister one day. "If there's something wrong with an idea, Jerry will find it."

Our minister was not impressed. "What a terrible thing to say about a person," he concluded. Anybody can criticize and find fault with things. That doesn't take any talent at all. But to look for the good in people and situations — that takes character.

I'm not talking about the "Pollyanna" who is so engulfed in positive thinking she can't face up to the real problems of life. That type of "cheerfulness" is a sickness. A truly cheerful person faces reality but doen't let the bad things in life get him down. Dwelling on the negatives doesn't solve anything. Looking for hidden blessings can cover a multitude of problems. Jesus said that, "In the world you are under pressure; but be confident! I have overcome the world" (John 16:33). Nothing happens to you—not even the greatest heartaches—that God cannot turn into a blessing if you will let Him.

A cheerful attitude is contagious. "A happy heart makes the face look sunny . . ." (Proverbs 15:13).

Are you a cheerful person? Do you look for the good in people and situations? Or are you continually criticizing someone or something? If you find yourself in the habit of criticizing, stop for a moment and think about what Christ has done for you. Make a list of all the good things He has given you and done for you. Now, then, what right have you to be critical and ungrateful about anything? Make a conscious effort to stop criticizing and start turning your sunny side up. That conscious effort is a beautiful form of prayer, for it speaks to God of your desire to change. And in His time He will give you the wisdom and love that produce His works in you.

Are you fun to know? Do people enjoy being around you? If the real you is all bottled up inside, let it out. Be yourself—the you God created you to be.

> *The will of God grows on you.*
> *That which is of God will fasten it-*
> *self on you and overpower and*
> *possess your entire being. That*
> *which is not of God will die—you*
> *will lose interest. But the plan of*
> *God will never die. The thing*
> *God wants you to do will become*
> *stronger each day in your thoughts,*
> *in your prayers, in your planning.*
> *It grows and grows!*
>
> **DAVID WILKERSON**

4

What in the World Are You Doing?

You and Your Job

During her single years, Margo's enjoyment of her nursing career was obvious. Always happy and cheerful with her patients, she had many opportunities to share Christ.

When I met Janet she was an elevator operator and embarrassed about it. "She doesn't want anyone to know what she does," a friend confided.

Why was one girl happy in her job and another not? Is there something wrong with being an elevator operator? Of course not. The key lies in each girl's attitude toward her work.

The single years offer unlimited opportunities to pursue meaningful work goals. You are free to travel when and where you wish. With a little scrimping here and there you can get as much schooling as you need or want. You can choose the kind of work you most enjoy with less thought about salary and location because you don't have to help support five children or pay off a thirty-year mortgage on the house. You are free as a bird (within the bounds of God's will for your life) to choose a profession that interests you and advance in it.

Why, then, are there Janets in this world who don't like their jobs and make sure other people know it?

Some girls have a one-track mind which hinders their enjoyment of anything else. They want to get married. Period. Nothing but marriage interests them. A job is a necessary evil to keep from starving to death until a husband comes along. All their thoughts and energies are channeled toward dreaming about the day when they will marry.

"Just the other day I was asked what my ambition in life was," writes a twenty-six-year-old woman. "This started me thinking, and I answered quite bluntly that it was to get married, settle down, and raise a family. I've never felt settled in anything that I've done yet. I'm one confused kid and have always felt that I'm just filling in time and space, and that someday I'd find what I was looking for if I kept trying different things.

"Don't mistake me," she continues, "I am waiting for the Lord to lead. I'm not going to jump into marriage until I find the right one. But no men are in sight yet so I must continue to fill in time and space."

If God wants you to marry, then marriage for you is a worthy goal. But not if it causes you to lose interest in everything else in life. Involvement in a meaningful occupation prior to marriage can help prepare you to be a good mate. Through your job you can learn new skills, gain new knowledge, meet new and interesting people, and share your faith with others. Suppose you do marry and suddenly find yourself widowed or divorced. Many a woman has wished she had job training and experience to fall back on when she suddenly finds herself the sole support of the family. The girl with the one-track mind for marriage misses out on the important things a good job can contribute to her life. Buried in those ever-present dreams of matrimony she may even miss out on some very important dates. No man is impressed with a girl whose only topic of conversation is matrimony. In fact it will probably frighten him away!

Let's face it. A job is also a status symbol. A married woman's status is determined largely by who she's married to. A single woman's status is determined by what she does for a living.

There are many reasons why a woman may be dissatisfied with her job. And some of them are perfectly legitimate. Perhaps you have taken a job for which you are underqualified (causing frustration) or overqualified (causing boredom). If so, take the additional training needed to become qualified or look around for something more challenging. The important thing is to *enjoy* what you are doing.

Your attitude toward your work tells a lot about you as a person. If you enjoy your work, your happiness will radiate to others. If you dislike your work, your negative attitude will spread like wildfire. First you hate your job. Then you begin to dislike the people with whom you work. Pretty soon you become sarcastic, critical, and perhaps even downright rude. And eventually your attitude will spread to your friends and even the men you date. You may purr like a kitten when you're around that man you want to impress, but sooner or later he'll find out how you treat the people at work. When he learns you don't like your job he's going to wonder why.

"If you are miserable or bored in your work," says Bruce Larson in his book *Dare to Live Now,* "or dread going to it, then God is speaking to you. He either wants to change the job you are in — or — more likely — He wants to change *you.*"

If you are unhappy with your job, ask yourself a few questions.

1. *Is the work interesting and challenging?* Do you look forward to going to work in the morning (well, *most* mornings, anyway)? Or do the eight hours at work seem like an eternity?

If boredom is the theme, chances are you are capable of much more than the job offers. Are there other jobs in the company that would be more interesting? Why not apply for them? Or perhaps you'd rather be in a different line of work altogether. Find out what kind of training is necessary and go

after it. Forty hours a week is a lot of time to spend doing something you hate. If sheer laziness is your only excuse for not
pursuing more interesting work, shame on you!

2. *Is the salary adequate?* If salary is your only consideration in looking for a job, you'll be in big trouble. At the same
time, however, the Bible says the workman is worthy of his
hire. There is no reason why you should settle for a mediocre
salary if the same job at a better salary is available.

My first year and a half out of college I worked as secretary
to the department head of a Christian institution. My salary
was pitifully low. Even with minimal expenses I went in the
hole financially every month. I appealed to my boss and to his
boss for a raise in pay but neither was able to give it to me. I
was perfectly willing to live "on faith," but the seriousness of
my financial condition finally convinced me that that was not
the kind of faith God wanted me to live on. I quit my job and
got a secretarial position with a company that paid a substantially higher salary. Because of the increased income I was
able to save enough money to allow me to tackle graduate
school a year and a half later.

3. *Does the work you are doing dishonor Christ in any way?*
Is your company laced with shady dealings? There are few
companies in this world that are 100 percent honest. But for
the most part, a company is either on the up and up or it isn't.
Are you ever asked to juggle the books, lie to customers, or
pad reports with misinformation? If so, it is not likely God
would want you to remain in such an organization.

4. *Are you in God's will to the best of your ability?* Margo's
love for her work and her Christian testimony to her patients
was obvious evidence that she was in God's will. Janet's
attitude toward her job as an elevator operator, however,
indicated something was wrong. Perhaps it was a matter of
pride, a feeling that "I'm too good for this kind of job." In
that case maybe God was trying to teach her something about
humility. Perhaps she was just too lazy to take whatever training was necessary to find a more enjoyable job. It is also possible that she had simply never accepted the fact that this was

the place in which God wanted her to serve Him. A cheerful elevator operator who radiates the love of Christ can have a tremendous influence on the people she serves, especially in an office building where she meets the same people day after day. But to have that kind of ministry she must willingly accept the fact that this is God's place of service for her—at least until He shows her something else. The cheerfulness that makes her a good operator may also help her move up the ladder when a more challenging job becomes available.

If you are unhappy with your job or are simply filling in time at a job until Mr. Right comes along, take a good long look at yourself. Either you or your job needs to change.

Let's assume now that you've found a job you really like. Just what does it take to be successful on the job and move up the company ladder?

Someone has suggested that to be successful in business a woman must be able to look like a woman, act like a lady, and think like a man! And there's a great deal of truth in that simple statement. The way in which a woman conducts herself in the business world is vitally important to her Christian testimony and her role as a woman.

Look Like a Woman

—An important part of looking like a woman is just that—looking like a *woman.* Today's casual styles often make it difficult to tell the boys from the girls. Leave your blue jeans, sandals, and Indian headbands at home. Your boss will not be impressed if you dress like a hophead who just came down off a trip. Business-like suits and dresses are much more appropriate and always in style.

Dress as attractively as your budget will permit and keep your hair well groomed (clean and shiny!) in the style most becoming to you. Slim down if you're overweight. Fatten up if you're too thin. Take a good look in a full-length mirror every morning before you leave for the office. Be neat, clean, and as attractive as possible. Wear a light cologne so you'll smell nice. With the variety of hair stylists, makeup specialists, and fashion consultants available today, no woman has any excuse for not looking her very best.

Act Like a Lady

Avoid extremes in styles—short, short skirts, low necklines, layers and layers of ruffles. Be extra careful when you sit down. Today's short skirts make it next to impossible to sit down without showing the tops of your panty hose and more! Sit down in front of a mirror and you'll be shocked at the view the men in your office get even when you think your skirts are tucked around you. Practice until you can sit gracefully without providing a view—or else stick with maxis.

Be careful about office romances. Some organizations prohibit fraternization between employees. If this is the policy where you work, abide by it. And even if it isn't a policy, be careful. If you date a fellow employee and things don't work out, going to work can be pretty grim.

Contrary to popular opinion, it is not necessary to have an affair with your boss in order to get ahead. If it *is* necessary in your company, the job isn't worth it. (By the way, at some time or another you'll probably have a crush on your boss, but it will pass. If he's married, be *sure* it passes.)

Another area where a Christian woman has to be careful is in the area of "business dates"—having lunch or dinner with your boss or other married men in the company. A situation that once, no doubt, caused raised eyebrows is now quite commonplace and not necessarily bad. It all depends on the reason for such business dates.

Many business dates are a necessary part of the business world and need not be refused. Sometimes lunch or dinner is the only time left in a busy day to talk about important business. In such cases this is part of your job. However, do what you can to avoid dark intimate restaurants or other questionable situations which might cause talk. You have as much responsibility to protect your boss's reputation as to protect your own. If your boss starts telling you his wife doesn't understand him or makes advances, avoid such encounters in the future.

Think Like a Man

This, of course, is impossible and no man really wants you to. But you can and must be businesslike and professional like a man. When things go wrong, avoid emotional outbursts (anger or tears) which are quickly labeled "just like a woman." Men view the business world objectively, logically, and without emotion. Only at home with their wives do they reveal their true feelings and frustrations.

Keep your personal problems out of the office as much as possible. If you need to confide in someone, go to your minister or a close friend outside the office.

Be honest. Don't make off with pencils or paper clips or cheat on your time card. My husband recently told me that one of the things that attracted him to me was that he knew I never phoned in sick when I wasn't. You may think you're getting away with something, but eventually dishonesty takes its toll.

Some women constantly compete with men. You've probably seen the type. Perhaps their most outstanding quality is that they are domineering. And no man likes to be dominated by a woman. Their theme song is "equality." They'll raise a fuss if they don't get a raise they think is due them and complain of discrimination against women. (I watched a woman being interviewed on television one day who was the president of an organization to prevent discrimination against women. When the moderator of the show asked how many ladies in the audience would join such an organization, only three raised their hands!) [A woman who carries the torch for equality may gain the position or raise, but in the process she loses a very precious commodity which only women possess—femininity.]

Now don't get me wrong. I'm all for women moving ahead in the business world. If God has given you talents in a specific area, by all means move ahead in your field. The ladder of success was meant to be climbed by women as well as men. Just be careful how you climb that ladder. If you climb it at the expense of a man's ego, I wonder if it was worth the trip.

Despite some of the commendable efforts of women's libbers, it is still possible you may not make as much money as a man in a position similar to yours. And you may not receive as many promotions as he does either. But is that just cause to throw up your defenses and start campaigning bitterly for equality? It just may be that your attitude is what's holding you back from a promotion, not the fact that you are a woman. If your company is hard-nosed about promoting women, move on to a company where you will have more freedom.

Don't talk too much. Men hate gabby women. This includes gossiping which is a deadly pastime. Remember Thumper, the rabbit? He always used to say, "If you can't say something good about somebody, don't say nuthin' at all." It also includes general office chitchat which is unnecessary and distracting. Coffee breaks and lunch hours are for socializing. In between keep unnecessary talk at a minimum.

Keep company secrets. If your boss tells you something in confidence, don't open your mouth. And don't discuss your company's shortcomings outside the company. If you don't like the company, go somewhere else. Don't take out your frustrations by unloading its faults on others. [Loyalty is an important commodity on the path to success.]

The key word here is to be *feminine*. This does not mean layering yourself in ruffles or dousing yourself in perfume ad nauseam. It simply means being the woman God made you to be.

One of the most successful professional women I know is an executive editor in a Christian publishing house. She has an amazing ability to direct traffic without being the slightest bit domineering—to be businesslike and still be feminine. She can guide a discussion so unobtrusively you hardly know she's doing it. She accomplishes what she set out to accomplish, but in the process you are scarcely aware that you are being *led* by a woman. I think this must be particularly appealing to the men who work under her.

Suppose a co-worker is three weeks late getting a report in to you. And you can't make up the final report without his. What do you do?

You could say, "Jim, I've been waiting three weeks for your report and I've just about had it. Now get that thing in here by 5:00 P.M. or I'm going to make things hot for you."

A better way I found is, "Jim, I know you are a terribly busy man. Is there any way I can help you get your report finished?" He was so pleased at the compliment ("you're a busy man") and the understanding ("Is there any way I can help?") that the material I needed was written and on my desk before I knew it!

Or suppose you have a really great idea for improving one of your company's products. A male co-worker has a different idea. If you really think your idea is better than his, you could battle things through like a bull moose until you get your way. Or you could present the case for your idea, listen carefully to his idea, and then say, "You could be right about that, Doug. I'll leave that decision up to you" (if the decision is his to make). By taking the pressure off him you leave him free to choose whichever idea he prefers. If your suggestion is better, chances are he will use it — and be grateful for your good ideas.

In the long run, you will never lose out by being feminine.

Let's Take Stock

	Most of the time	Rarely or never

Check the appropriate answer in the columns on the right.

1. Do you look forward to going to work each day?
2. Is your work challenging and interesting?
3. Do you view your job as a place where you can serve God?
4. Do you look for opportunities to share Christ with your coworkers?
5. Are you in God's will to the best of your knowledge?

	Yes	No

6. Have you gotten a raise within the last five years?
7. Have you gotten a promotion within the last five years?

If most of your check marks fall in the right-hand column, it's time to take stock of both you and your job.

If I am unhappy in my job, why have I not made any effort to change?

What new knowledge or skills would I need to secure a more challenging job?

What am I going to do about it?

5

Making Ends Meet —
When They Don't

You and Your Money

Payday is one week off. You have 7¢ in your checking account and $1.00 in your purse. What do you do?

A. Cash in your empty pop bottles
B. Ask your boss for an advance
C. Write home for money
D. Buy something

If you chose *D* for your answer, you're obviously a woman after my own heart. *B* and *C* are out of the question since they only put you further in debt. *A* is okay for *real* emergencies. But when you're only in semi-desperate straits, buying something somehow gives you hope for the future. At least it does me. An important rule of thumb, however, is never to spend more than half of your assets. A 50¢ magazine will just about do it. (How much of an emergency can you meet with the 57¢ that is left? Just about the same as with $1.07!)

The love of money is the root of all evil. And the management of money isn't far behind. As the saying goes, "Why is there always so much month left at the end of the money?" Seems like no matter how you try, there's never enough money to meet all your expenses. Today's inflationary prices aren't helping any.

The best way to find out where your money goes is to do a little paper work. Make a list of all of your expenses – weekly, monthly, and yearly. Include your rent, church and charity giving, food, automobile, insurance, clothing, recreation, gifts, and other items. Total your expenses for an entire year and then divide by twelve to determine how much you are spending month by month.

The next step is to work out a reasonable budget. If you don't *plan* how your money is to be spent, your expenses will fall into place of their own accord. Instead of you controlling your expenses, however, your expenses will end up controlling you.

Let's look at some of the major items in your budget.

Tithe   The first place to begin when you set up your budget is with the money you choose to return to the Lord. All that you have is a gift from Him. The Bible makes very clear that under the law, one-tenth of all that you have belongs to Him. It does not belong to you. And to hang onto it is to actually rob from God.

However, since we are under grace rather than law, a tenth is the very least we should give to God. What you give over and above a tithe is real giving. If you give grudgingly out of a sense of duty, you might as well not give at all, for "God loves a cheerful giver." Once you decide to put God first in your giving, you will probably find it easier to put Him first in other areas of your life as well.

Savings   Force yourself to save or you will never save a cent. I know from experience how easy it is to let money slip through your fingers on things that seem so very worthwhile at the time. And in a year or so you have little to show for your spending except a collection of debts. Just as you set aside a tenth (or more) of your income for God, deduct another 10 percent for your savings account. Figure the rest of your budget within the remaining 80 percent.

Rent   One of the largest chunks of your income will probably be what you spend on rent. If you grew up in a very nice home, you will no doubt want at least the same standard of living when you venture out on your own for the first time. But remember, your earning power at age eighteen or twenty-two will probably in no way be comparable to that of your middle-aged father who has worked for years to reach his present standard of living. A plush apartment for which you pay through the nose is hardly a wise investment of your money. A roommate to share expenses is usually the best way to make ends meet.

As time goes on you may decide that you'd like to invest that rent money in property you can call your own. A condominium might be a good investment if you'd rather not have to worry about upkeep.

Select carefully the area in which you will live. Don't choose a house or apartment in an area of the city that is especially unsafe, just because the rent is cheap. And while we're talking about safety, let me suggest a few things I think are especially important for the single woman.

The next time you hear of a woman being beaten, raped, or murdered, read all you can about the incident. This may sound like a sordid assignment, but there's a reason for it. In almost every newspaper account I've read (if not all of them) the reporter has mentioned some precaution the woman failed to take. She left a bedroom window wide open. Or she left the door unlocked. She went for a walk in the park alone late at night. Or she left a bar alone at night and jumped into her unlocked car without checking the back seat. Read — and profit from the mistakes of others.

Be sure your apartment is reasonably burglar proof before you move in. Second-floor apartments make window breaking more difficult than ground-floor apartments, unless a walkway runs the full length of the building. Do the windows have screens that lock? Do the windows lock tightly? One apartment I lived in for several months had a louvered glass window a few inches from the front door. All it took to break in (and I did it many times when I didn't have my key) was to slip out the screen, remove one louver, reach in, and twist the doorknob. If at all possible, have a night latch on every outside door and a peephole so you can look out but nobody can look in.

Keep your apartment or house locked when you're in it as well as when you're away. If it's too hot in the summer to keep the doors closed, find an apartment with screen doors that lock. A locked screen door lets the air in and at least puts up a temporary block for a burglar. Close and lock the door before you go to bed.

Never open your door at night unless you know who is on the outside. And it had better be someone you know well—your mother, your best friend, your minister. Don't let a salesman get one foot in the door. Many an unsuspecting woman has been raped, beaten, or even murdered simply because she opened a door she should have kept closed. Ask your friends to telephone before they come over.

If an intruder enters your home or apartment during the night, your best bet is usually to pretend to be asleep. If a man is there to molest you, however, you may have to use other tactics. One girl I read about calmly talked to the man. She kept up a steady dialogue, appealing to his pride by asking why such a good-looking man as he had to go around breaking into homes. The more she talked the more his passion subsided and he finally left the house without harming her.

Never list your first name in the telephone directory. Use one or both initials. A single woman's name listed openly in the phone directory makes her a prey to any phone nut who decides to dial her number. And don't forget—if they have your phone number they also have your address. If you list only your initials you may end up on the mailing list of every men's clothing store in town. But throwing away junk mail is easier than trying to trace crank phone calls.

Be careful to whom you give your address and phone number. One divorced woman I once knew joined a social group and let her name and address be placed in the group's printed directory. She was horrified one day to find the directory tacked to a telephone pole at a bus stop. Shortly after that a man caught her as she was going into her apartment and forced his way in. As calmly as possible she let him sit down and began to talk to him in an attempt to sidetrack him from his obvious intent. He told her many things about herself that a stranger wouldn't ordinarily know. Fortunately, something or somebody scared him away before he did any harm. But the woman felt sure he must have found her through the bus-stop copy or another copy of that directory.

When you join any kind of a group, be sure you know the purpose and membership well before you allow your name to be placed in a directory. Even then you can't control who gets a copy of that directory.

Never put your first name on your mailbox. List only your last name or initials and last name.

Food Your health is your most important possession and what you eat determines in large measure just how healthy you will be. If you're constantly on the go, the line of least resistance is to skip a meal, grab a snack here and there, or live on a diet of hamburgers and coffee. If you live alone, there usually isn't much incentive to fix first-rate meals just for yourself.

Eating in restaurants all the time is pretty expensive and robs you of the opportunity to learn how to be a really good cook. At least part of the way to a man's heart is definitely through his stomach. Force yourself to fix and eat well-balanced meals. With careful planning you can eat well on even a small food budget.

Automobile One of the most expensive items in your budget is your automobile — if you own one. Owning and operating a car is a big investment. And with the predictions of a serious gas shortage, the cost will probably continue to climb.

Before you jump into any car purchase, ask yourself if you really need one. If you live in a city where mass transit is available, an automobile may be a luxury you really can't afford. In his bachelor days, a friend of ours decided to beat the system and save some money. He sold his car and for two years relied totally upon the bus system or his feet for transportation. (In Los Angeles that isn't easy.) He found the experiment highly rewarding — financially and otherwise.

When he married a couple of years ago, his wife's car became the family automobile. A new decision faced him, however— whether or not to buy an inexpensive second car for him to use going to and from work. He figured the cost and discovered a second car would cost him about $1500 a year to own and operate. He opted in favor of the bus which costs him $270 a year.

Total up the amount of money you spend per month on gas and oil, car payments, insurance and repairs, and you will discover that a large portion of your paycheck is eaten up by your car. Consider the possibility of selling your car and using the bus. (You meet more people when you ride public transportation than when you travel all alone in a car.)

Think through the areas of the city where you travel the most and study the bus or subway lines that serve those areas. Then find an apartment that is close to one of those lines and also close to shopping and laundry facilities. The few times you really need a car you can always rent one. Although the cost of renting a car may be high, you will save money in the long run.

If you do not know how to drive, by all means take driving lessons and learn how. I think it is very important for a woman to be able to drive—as a single woman and after she is married. This is one area where being a "helpless Hannah" is not necessarily a good idea. Emergency situations may arise when it is essential that you know how to drive.

Selecting a car is often difficult for a single woman—particularly if you are buying a used car. Those of us who buy cars by color, size, or the number of accessories often learn to our dismay that what's up front is a lot more important than the paint job.

Don't buy a big fancy car unless you are rolling in money. A big car whose maintenance cost is high and gas mileage low is a poor investment and will keep you perpetually broke. Stick to the smaller and less expensive compact cars that are cheaper to operate.

When you buy a car, especially a used car, take someone with you who understands the inner workings of the automobile. Your father, brother, or a friend will probably be glad to help you select a model that runs well and is within your budget.

To help you purchase a new car at a reasonable price, an organization called Car/Puter International Corp. (1603 Bushwick Avenue, Brooklyn, New York 11207) will be of help. For a fee of $7.95 Car/Puter will send you their current New Car Yearbook and a list of all the options and accessories available for the make and model of car in which you are interested. You check off the accessories you want and return the list to Car/Puter. They will send you a computerized print-out listing both the dealer price and the retail price for each item and whatever freight and dealer charges might be involved. You may find to your surprise that a car which costs the dealer about $3300 may be selling for as much as $4200.

You can use the Car/Puter print-out to make the best deal possible with your local car dealer. But if he won't meet the price you offer, or if you'd rather not go to all that trouble, you can simply use your print-out form as a purchase order, and order the car directly through Car/Puter. You pay only $125 over dealer cost for most cars and you get the same new-car warranty and servicing as if you had personally negotiated with the dealer.

Learn something about your car. Take a course in auto mechanics (yes, women take them, too) or ask a friend for help. It won't strain your femininity to learn how to change the oil or a tire. Changing the oil will save you a little money and knowing how to change a tire may come in mighty handy if you are stranded somewhere and nobody comes to your rescue.

One of the big costs of owning an automobile is auto insurance. Contact several insurance agencies and compare prices. Consider insurance costs before you buy a car. Your age, and the age, make, and model of the car are important factors. So is the area in which you live. Our insurance skyrocketed when we moved from one part of the Los Angeles area to another.

The bane of every woman car owner's existence is trying to find a reliable mechanic to repair her car. Since most of us know very little about automobiles, we are the prey of any unscrupulous mechanic who wants to make a fast buck (or a couple of hundred bucks!).

There is no sure way that I know of to find a reliable mechanic except through trial and error. Here again friends can be a help. Ask around and see who your friends recommend. Once you find a mechanic you can trust, stick with him till death do you part. A mechanic who sees you regularly will probably be less inclined to gyp you than one who has never seen you before and will never see you again.

When you travel be especially careful of service-station attendants who tell you that you need a new fan belt, your radiator cleaned out, or some other repair when all you did was stop for gas. An attendant with a razor blade hidden between his fingers can slit your fan belt without your knowing it and then tell you that you need a new one. If he places two fingers below the handle when he inserts the dip stick, the oil mark will be lower on the stick than it should be. If you tell him to add oil he may use a can that is actually empty—and charge you for the oil he didn't put in.

When you stop for gas or repairs, get out of the car and watch what goes on under the hood. You may not know a battery from a spark plug. But the mechanic doesn't know that. He'll be less inclined to pull any funnies if you're watching every move he makes. If he tells you something is definitely wrong with your car, thank him and then drive to another station or two for a consensus of opinion before you have any work done.

And now for a few safety rules regarding the use of your car.

Always lock your car when it is parked and when you are in it. Even when you are driving in broad daylight, keep the doors locked. Always check the back seat of your car before getting in. Many tragedies occur when a woman carelessly hops into a car without checking the back seat, only to find moments later a gun at her neck or a hand on her shoulder.

Never walk anywhere alone at night in a big city. Even on a well-lighted street. Go by car if your car is parked close to your apartment, or by bus if the bus stop is nearby. If neither of these is available, wait until daylight. Your safety is more important than whatever you thought you needed at the store.

Health insurance No matter how small your income, one item you must not overlook is health insurance. You may not enjoy paying the monthly premiums when you're in good health, but if you get sick you'll be mighty glad you did. If the company you work for does not provide health insurance, investigate Blue Cross, Blue Shield, or another plan that meets your needs.

Life insurance Who would pay for the funeral expenses if you were to die tomorrow? Maybe you've never given that much thought, but it's time you did. A policy that at least covers burial expenses would be a big help to whomever becomes responsible for your affairs after your demise.

Credit Buying

If your wallet looks anything like most people's you are well stocked with credit cards. In some ways they are a valuable piece of plastic. In many ways they are the curse of our society.

Credit cards are good for emergencies and for identification purposes. But for most of our buying they are a definite liability. Why? Because they encourage us to live far above our means.

A credit card allows you to:

Buy what you can't afford.
Spend money you don't have and may never have (what if you get laid off?).
Pay as much as 18 percent interest on unpaid balances.
Keep yourself continually in debt.

If you use a credit card wisely it can be your friend. Never charge more than you can pay off in a lump sum when your next bill comes in. If you have to make a large purchase which you can't pay off all at once, take out a loan at the bank where the interest will be substantially lower than that charged by the department store. If you really want to put an end to splurge buying, tear up all of your credit cards except one. Save that one for identification purposes and for dire emergencies.

You and Your Uncle

For many years single taxpayers have been paying dearly on April 15. Fortunately, steps are being taken to correct this unnecessary financial "penalty" for being single. An organization called CO$T (Committee of Single Taxpayers, P.O. Box 1789, Washington, D.C. 20013) is working for tax equality regardless of one's marital status. Drop them a note if you'd like to get involved. With a little effort and study you can ease some of the financial strain and still remain friends with Uncle Sam.

Retirement

At age twenty-five the idea of saving up and investing for your retirement may seem decidedly remote. Most of us figure that pretty soon we'll get married and then we won't have to worry about a retirement income. Friend husband will take care of all that.

But suppose you don't marry. Or you marry and are widowed with no provisions for your retirement. Financial planning at fifty-five or sixty is a little late. There are several ways you can plan for your retirement. Let's take a look at some.

Social Security A guaranteed income when you retire sounds like smooth sailing. But frequent articles in the newspapers indicate that it is just about impossible to live on social security alone. Therefore, it is vitally necessary that you make additional financial provisions for your retirement.

Pensions When you take a job, inquire about the retirement plan provided by the company. Some companies provide healthy pension plans, some provide none. Maybe you won't stay with the same company long enough to take advantage of their plan. But then again maybe you will.

Investments One of the easiest ways to invest your money is through a mutual funds plan. You can invest a little or a lot and the company will handle your money for you. When you retire your original investment plus the money it has made for you through the years is available to you in a lump sum or in monthly installments.

If you're interested in learning about the stock market, a number of books are available to help you tell the difference between the bulls and the bears. If you have only a small amount to invest, you might want to join an investment club where each person's money is pooled to buy shares and you learn how to buy. Talk to a stockbroker and ask him about an investment club you could join, or ask him to do your investing for you.

Savings   Consider your savings account as a cushion fund for the present and future, but not necessarily as a source of retirement income. The interest paid by a bank is low in comparison to the earning power your money will have if you invest.

These are a few of the retirement plans available. As you assess your financial future you will discover other ways. The important thing is to start planning now for your future. None of these plans will be a waste of money even if you do marry in the meantime.

Ten Money-Saving Tips

And now for a few tips on how to make and save a little money:

1. Do your Christmas shopping in January and August when the white sales are on. Watch other sales during the year, also, and you can do most of your gift buying at a fraction of the full price. Be sure the items you buy are something the person does not have or, if buying clothing, that the item will fit. Sale items usually can't be returned.

2. Buy clothing at the end of the season when it is on sale and save it for next year. Avoid extremely faddish items that may not be in style next year.

3. Clip coupons that offer 5¢, 10¢ or 25¢ off or cash refunds on food and household items. Save the amount deducted from the price or you will never benefit from the coupons. I collect my "cold hard cash" coupon money in a jar in the refrigerator (if you were a burglar would you look in the refrigerator for money?) and use it primarily for birthday and Christmas presents for my husband.

4. One way to save money on your grocery bill is to comparison shop. However, this takes time that you as a working girl may not have. If you don't have the time to shop in several stores, watch for sales and special discounts in the store where you do shop. For example, house brands are usually cheaper than name

brands and taste just as good. A large sign may announce that a certain name brand is on special for 27¢ a can. Right next to it you discover the house brand is only 25¢.

5. With the high price of meat you would do well to learn how to use some of the less expensive proteins. For example, cheese, canned tuna, and kidney beans provide necessary protein at considerably lower cost than expensive cuts of beef and pork.

6. Have a garage sale. Clean out all the old junk you want to get rid of: clothing, jewelry, funiture, dishes, etc. It helps sometimes if you have an antique or two to throw in as bait. Put up a sign or run an ad in the newspaper. Ask friends and neighbors to go in with you if you don't have much to sell. I picked up $90 in a garage sale once and unloaded a lot of junk I wanted to get rid of.

7. Take advantage of other people's garage and patio sales. I recently bought a luscious lavender straw hat with a floppy brim for 50¢ (it had never been worn), a brown basket with a hinged lid for 15¢ which looks great on the hearth with a potted plant in it, and a large, much needed garment bag for $1.00. Thrift stores are another source of good buys. Discipline yourself not to buy things you don't need just because they're cheap. Look for items you actually need and you'll be surprised how inexpensively you can furnish your apartment or clothe your body.

8. If you're really in a financial bind, consider moonlighting, but only with short hours or for a short period of time. If you work at a "think" job all day, choose a moonlight job that doesn't require much thinking. Don't moonlight for long. It isn't worth the damage to your health. And it won't help your date life either when you say, "I'd love to see you sometime, Jim, but I'm only free between 2:30 and 4:00 on Thursday afternoons."

9. Turn a hobby into a profit-maker. If needlecraft, pottery, or candlemaking is your specialty, perhaps your local handcraft shop will sell your things on consignment. If you've always wanted to be a writer or an artist, take some night classes and give it a try. Nothing ventured, nothing gained. You just might discover some hidden talent you didn't know you had.

10. Join a book club and take advantage of the introductory

offer. Use the discount and introductory books for gifts or to build up your own library. Choose a club which has enough books you need or want to make joining worthwhile. A $7.95 book that sells for $5.95 through the club may not be a bargain after all, if you discover the same book in paperback at the local bookstore for $1.25. We recently joined a special interest book club. For joining the club we will receive three books whose retail prices total $46.95. We pay only 99¢ per book. My father doesn't know it yet, but he's going to receive one of those books for a Christmas present. It retails for $13.50.

Live Below Your Means

A divorced friend suggests that instead of not living beyond your means you should not even live up to your means. In other words, don't spend every cent you have. Set your standard of living *below* what you actually could afford. In today's economy that isn't easy, but it is possible if you are willing to make some sacrifices here and there.

Why should you try to live below your means? She suggests several reasons. There is a sense of freedom in knowing that you could spend more if you wanted to. The person who barely scrapes by from paycheck to paycheck hardly feels secure. When you live below your means you then have opportunity to expand yourself as a person. Use the extra money for travel, preparation for retirement, music lessons, a lecture series, and for other things that are a worthwhile investment of your time and money.

This same friend tells of the time she had to leave her job out West for a job in the East. She did not look forward to the adjustment from a warm climate to a bitterly cold one. In fact she didn't want to take the job at all. But she knew that was where God wanted her and so she went. After she moved she bought herself a gift — a beautiful fur coat. And whenever people asked about her coat she told them it was "a gift to me from myself." While the coat represented a healthy investment, it was not money ill-spent. The coat was lighter weight and warmer than a cloth coat and outwore several cloth coats in the long run — plus the added factor of a pleasant boost to her morale. It matched everything and always looked elegant. The point is, however, she was obviously not living up to her means or she could never have afforded such a happy gift.

Perhaps this is a little of what Jesus meant when He told us, ". . . do not worry about your living,—what you are to eat (or drink), or about your body, what you are to wear" (Matthew 6:25). One of the ways God provides for us is by giving us the good sense to know how to manage our money. The person who barely makes it from payday to payday or lives beyond his means takes plenty of thought about what he will eat, drink, and wear. Worrying about your finances is time-consuming and an emotional drain. There will be times when all of us must give serious attention to our financial condition. But in the long run I think many of our worries could be eliminated if we actually lived below our means.

Put God first in every aspect of your financial affairs. Ask Him to give you the wisdom to manage your finances wisely. When I go shopping I frequently ask God to show me the things I should buy and keep me from buying the things I shouldn't. It's a great way to reduce frivolous spending.

6

Person-to-Person

How to Live With Your Roommate

In my thirty-two single years I somehow managed to accumulate a grand total of sixteen roommates. Not all at the same time, thank heaven, but not all one-at-a-time either. First there were my four college roommates. Today one is happily married, one is a widow, and two are still single. The twelve that followed included one who was mentally unbalanced, two who leaned toward lesbianism, and one who married very unwisely and is probably divorced by now. My last two roommates and several more before them were wonderful Christian women and are among my closest friends today.

The longest I ever lived with a roommate was four years. The shortest was about one week. I also lived alone for nearly two years. Most of the women were easy to get along with. From the few who weren't I learned a lot.

The utmost in freedom is to live alone and some girls prefer this. You can sleep until noon, play the stereo at 3 A.M., take the trash out when you feel like it—and there's nobody around to complain. However, most of us find living alone rather lonely and prefer having a roommate.

Economic factors make it imperative for most women to share the rent with at least one other living body. That gorgeous apartment with the pool and sun deck suddenly becomes a possibility when you find someone else with enough shekels to match yours.

A good roommate also provides a certain amount of companionship. If you feel like having a hamburger at 11 P.M., the two of you can pile in the car and head for the nearest McDonald's. This companionship is not always so important to men. One of my roommates dated a man (I'll call him Bob) who had a roommate (Jim). Apparently the two men rarely if ever saw or communicated with each other because one time Jim asked my roommate for a date. Circumstances were such that my roommate was quite sure Jim had no idea she was steadily dating *his* roommate! My husband had a roommate for about six years before we got married. Though they remain good friends today they rarely spent much time together. Each was busy with his own life. For a girl, however, a good roommate can help ease the loneliness on a Saturday night when neither of you has a date.

In addition to the economic and companionship factors, you can learn a lot about how to get along with people (including a husband some day) by living with another woman. The give-and-take relationship you develop with your roommate will carry over to your future relationship with a husband. If you can't get along with a roommate, how will you ever get along with a husband? Don't think for a moment that "everything will change" when you finally get a ring on your finger. Nonsense! If you're a witch to live with now you'll be a witch to live with when you get married. Develop a good relationship with your roommate and you're well on your way toward becoming the kind of person who can live together in harmony with a husband.

The first step toward a good roommate relationship is to pick one you know. Moving in with a total stranger can be disastrous. One of my best roommates arrived sight unseen and we got along fine, though we were never bosom buddies. But my four worst experiences were with girls I had never met or knew only by sight.

A certain amount of compatibility is required if sharing an apartment is going to be successful. If you already know the other girl, you know whether or not you have similar interests and ideas. Is she a fastidious housekeeper while you tend to shovel out once a year before your mother comes? Does she like to throw loud parties while you prefer a quiet evening listening to the stereo with a couple of friends? If your likes and dislikes are too extreme you may find living together a real grind.

Once you've found a suitable roommate, the best way to avoid problems is to prevent them. And the most likely potential problem centers around KP and cleaning duty. Who's going to cook the meals and do the dishes? Who's going to vacuum the rugs and clean the bathroom? Set up a schedule as soon as you move in together.

One of my roommates was a schoolteacher who left earlier in the morning than I did and got home earlier in the afternoon. So I cooked breakfast and she cooked dinner. My first year of graduate school I had two roommates and each of us had a different class and work schedule. Our arrangement that year was for each person to do her own grocery shopping, cooking, and dish washing—which worked out better than I anticipated since one girl was a health-food addict whose idea of a good dinner consisted of sitting on the kitchen floor eating rose hips. With my last two roommates we all took assigned duties for one week at a time: one cooked and washed dishes, one vacuumed and dusted, one cleaned the floors and the bathrooms. Two weeks of not having to cook or wash dishes was heaven!

The most important thing in establishing a good relationship with your roommate is to treat her with respect. Would you like someone banging doors at 2 A.M. when you're trying to sleep? Of course not. Then try tiptoeing in after your next date. When you finish that midnight snack, wash your dishes and put them away. Don't let dishes pile up in the sink or expect your roommate to clean up after you.

What does the bathroom look like after you've bathed or dressed for a date? Is there water all over the floor? Rollers strewn everywhere? Long black hairs in the sink? The Golden Rule was never more applicable. Treat her the way you'd like her to treat you.

Despite your best efforts at roommateship, some day you may

end up with a lemon. *You* are the model roommate, but *she* is absolutely unbearable. What do you do?

First of all take a good look at yourself. Are you sure she is entirely to blame? Maybe your expectations are a little too high. Do you absolutely demand that the apartment be spotlessly clean at all times? Do you disapprove of her friends and all of the men she dates? Maybe *you* are the one who needs to change, not her.

My first year in college I was very conservative (no makeup back when no makeup was not in style) and a bit hard-nosed about some of my roommate's practices which I considered "worldly." One time when she was listening to the radio a song came on the air which I did not approve of. In no uncertain terms I let her know that I didn't want *that* kind of music playing in our room ever again. My performance was spectacular. And my roommate, bless her, did the best thing she could possibly have done. She moved out. I was crushed and fled in tears to the housemother and then home for the weekend for a little sympathy from my parents. When I returned to my dorm room on Sunday night, there was my roommate—moved back in. I had learned a valuable lesson and today we are very close friends.

If you and your roommate really are hopelessly incompatible, the best thing to do is part company. If she is living in your home (which is rarely the case) you can ask her to move. However, in most instances you will probably have to be the one to offer to leave. Moving is a traumatic experience, especially if you own your own furniture. But a new location can be much less traumatic than trying to stick it out with a roommate who drives you bananas.

And now a word about dating. Your roommate's dates, that is. Never, never, never date the same man your roommate is dating. If your roommate's boyfriend asks you for a date, decline politely. (You can decline any date without lying by saying you have previous plans. You *always* have a standing invitation to clean out your dresser drawers.) If he persists, tell him frankly that it is your policy not to date the same man your roommate dates. If he is more interested in you than in her, he may stop dating her in favor of you. After a reasonable length of time to observe your roommate in mourning you are then free to date him. At any rate he will respect you for your stand—and you'll avoid any knock-down-drag-outs with your roommate. Would you want her to date your boyfriend?

If your roommate invites her date over for dinner or asks him in for a cup of coffee after a date, give them both a pleasant hello and then disappear. In any roommate/date situation three is definitely a crowd. If curvature of the spine develops from reading or watching TV on the bed every night, plan to go somewhere on the nights your roommate wants to entertain.

Sooner or later the inevitable happens. Your roommate gets engaged. Unless you're a hopeless man-hater this is a tough blow for any girl. One of my roommates absolutely dropped me after she got married and I was terribly hurt. "Why go to all the work of developing a close friendship," I mourned, "if marriage is going to mean the end of it all?" Fortunately, my next roommate was not so self-centered. She and her husband took me out for pizza the day they got back from their honeymoon. They'll never know how much that meant to me.

When your roommate gets engaged it's hard not to feel terribly left out, especially if you aren't dating anyone at the moment. Satan will tempt you to feel jealous and lonelier than ever. Take steps immediately to prevent yourself from getting bogged down in self-pity. After that one bad experience I was better prepared the next time. When a very close friend (not a roommate) got engaged I knew that we would soon be able to spend very little time together. So I began building a friendship with another girl who was there to fill the gap when my friend got married.

Roommates to avoid:

• The clinging vine who wants to do *everything* with you. I'll never forget two sisters, both in their thirties. So far as I know, they still live together, attend the same church group together, participate in the same church activities together, and are always seen everywhere together. They always remind me of the phrase of that song that goes, "Lord, help the mister who comes between me and my sis!" Insecurity can drive two people together in a most unhealthy relationship. And the result can be disastrous to your date life.

• Lesbians. In my younger years I went through torture for several months living with two girls who were unnaturally attracted to each other. I was too naive and inexperienced to fully understand their problem, but I knew enough to know that some of the things going on between them were not normal. When I finally confided the situation to an objective person I realized that action had to be taken. One girl moved out of her own accord and the other one I eventually reported to someone who could help her.

• Women who are much older (fifteen to twenty years or more) or much younger than you. If you are both independent and maintain your own individual social lives, there's a reasonable chance you may get along. However, chances are you will have little in common. If you do enjoy living together, ask yourself why. Are you looking for a mother figure—an older woman to tell you what to do and when to do it? Or are you trying to *be* a mother figure with a daughter substitute to give you ego support?

• Any girl or woman who tends to drag you down morally and hinder you in your Christian growth. You have a Christian responsibility to your roommate, whether she is a Christian or a non-Christian. By the same token she has a responsibility to you. If one or the other of you fails in your responsibility, serious problems can result.

Is promiscuity a problem for you? Then the last person you should live with is a girl whose morals are loose. She will certainly not help you resist temptation and will probably only tear you down further. Whatever your area of temptation, the devil knows what it is and he will use any means possible to make you give in and sin—including your roommate. If you and your roommate are both Christians you should be able to share your problems, pray about them, and encourage one another in the Christian faith.

*Charm is deceitful and beauty is
passing, but a woman who reveres
the Lord will be praised.*

Proverbs 31:30

7

The Eyes Have It

How You Look and Act

As a Christian woman you have an important responsibility in
the way you look and act. For after all, you are a representative
of the King! That's a mighty high calling which deserves your
careful attention. The way you look and act can attract—or repel
—people from the One you represent.

Let's begin with your health.

I've Never Felt Better (Cough Cough)

As good stewards of God's gifts it is important that we take
care of our bodies—inside and out. That means regular checkups
with your doctor at least once a year. When you have your
checkup be sure to have the doctor do a pap smear. This test is
important because of the incidence of cancer of the female
organs among both single and married women. In between
checkups be sure to examine your breasts regularly for any signs
of growths that shouldn't be there. If just the thought of cancer
scares you half to death, remember that if it is detected early it
can often be arrested.

Good health also involves having your eyes checked every two
years and regular visits to the dentist. Cavity-ridden teeth are unattractive, can pour infection into your system, and certainly

65

don't contribute anything toward sweet-smelling breath. Visit your dentist at least once a year—and keep a bottle of mouthwash handy at home.

The most common complaint I hear when I suggest that someone go to the doctor is, "But that costs money," or "I can't afford to." My question is, "Can you afford *not* to?" Your health is a very important commodity given to you by God. Neglecting your body can lead to expensive doctor and dental bills and even permanent damage to your health.

Good health also includes proper rest and relaxation. Are you continually on the go? Hardly stopping long enough to take the next breath? Slow down. Know your own physical limitations and don't overdo. Jesus Christ is the Son of God, yet even He didn't try to meet everyone's needs. He took time out to rest and you must, too.

Few of us Americans ever get enough exercise. And we have flabby derrieres and pooched-out stomachs to prove it. We spend our days behind a desk and go home at night to sit out the rest of the evening in front of the TV. For good health you need to walk, swim, run, play tennis, bowl, or do exercises daily. Unless you're athletically inclined you will probably have to discipline yourself to get the proper exercise. Do you live within a mile or so of your work? Why not walk to work instead of driving or taking the bus?

And how about the food you eat? Do you eat well-balanced meals including plenty of fresh fruits and vegetables? Or do you clear out the pop bottles only when you hear your mother is coming and stock the refrigerator with milk (which you haven't drunk since you were eight), vegetables, and steak. You may fool your mother for a couple of days, but you aren't fooling your body. A well-balanced diet and proper exercise put color in your cheeks, a sparkle in your eye, and a spring in your walk.

Abigail Van Buren says a woman can't take a bath too often, and I heartily agree. One bath a day should be a minimum unless you're allergic to water. Use deodorant and other powders or lotions to keep you smelling clean and fresh between baths. Cleanliness, most assuredly, is next to godliness. There's something awfully wholesome and attractive about the well-scrubbed look. And now for the exterior you.

Hair Flair

Let's begin with your hair. Take a look in the mirror and what do you see? Soft silky locks attractively arranged? Or split ends and lackluster hair? Is your hairstyle becoming to you? Or is it a leftover from the 1950s? If you've been wearing the same hairstyle for many years, chances are you've grown so accustomed to it you may even think it is still in style.

Treat yourself to a trip to the beauty salon. I recommend a new hairstyle at least every two years to help keep yourself current and to give your morale a boost. Find a beautician who is creative in his or her work, not just one who cuts hair and rolls rollers. Friends whose hair always looks stunning can suggest someone to you. Tell her you want your hair styled and give her the freedom to experiment. Don't be afraid to try something new. And remember, a proper diet and frequent washings give you a head start on beautiful-looking hair.

Makeup Magic

A new hairstyle calls for a new look at your complexion. Is your face squeaky clean? Or do remnants of makeup (or dirt, heaven forbid) carry over day after day? If your skin is sallow and full of blemishes, here again an improper diet and lack of exercise may be the cause.

Whether or not you wear makeup and the amount you wear depends upon your own individual preferences. The no-makeup look is fine if you're young and have a super complexion. But most of us over thirty need a little help. If God had wanted us all to be raving beauties He would have made us that way. Instead He equipped us with the capacity to learn how to make ourselves look as attractive as possible.

Here let me say a word to those of you who do not wear makeup for religious reasons. If you honestly feel that makeup is wrong for you, then you shouldn't wear it. Too often, however, I think people place a taboo on wearing makeup (or jewelry) without really thinking through the reasons why.

When I was growing up, makeup was absolutely taboo because it was supposed to made women look "worldly." (Yes, I *know* Jezebel "painted her face," but her problem was much deeper than that.) Then along came the trend a few years later of not wearing any makeup at all. If what the world does in terms of makeup makes makeup worldly, then why didn't my Christian sisters start wearing makeup so they wouldn't look like the world? To be consistent it seems to me that's what they would have had to do.

One religious group refuses to wear wedding rings because a ring is considered "worldly." So the husband gives his wife a wristwatch instead. Why is a ring worldly but a watch is not? The problem is one of consistency. Whenever we lay down rules for specific things that are not spelled out in Scripture, we make it awfully difficult to be consistent in our beliefs.

A better way to establish our *do*'s and *don't*s, I think, is on the basis of the principles of Scripture. The Bible is explicit that we are to be modest (1 Timothy 2:9) and that we are to attract people to Christ (Philippians 1:20, 21), not call undue attention to ourselves. If anything you do calls undue attention to yourself, then it is not honoring to Christ. Too much makeup calls attention to yourself. So does no makeup if your face desperately needs a little color.

If you are unsure what kind of makeup is best for you, here again an expert can be of help. Visit the cosmetics specialist at a local department store and ask for help. Some cosmetic companies offer a free makeup job where you will learn what colors and kinds of makeup are best for you. Other cosmetics companies can also be of help. (Hint: When you apply foundation be sure to apply it to your neck as well as your face. Nothing is more unattractive than foundation that ends in a hard line at your chin.) The purpose of makeup should be to enhance your features. Avoid plastering it on like a mask.

The Flab Factor

From the neck up you're in great shape. But how about from the neck down? For years I ate anything I wanted and never worried a feather about my weight. But when I passed thirty the picture changed. I have now joined the ranks of the dieters. If your tummy (and a few other places!) have the bulges, make haste to rid yourself of those extra pounds. Fat is not attractive. Ask your doctor for a sensible diet and stick to it. And once you've shed those unnecessary pounds, remember that it is easier to maintain your weight than to take off twenty or thirty pounds.

The Rag Bag

And now let's take a look at your wardrobe. What kind of clothes do you put on your back day after day? Do the clothes you wear fit your image? Or are you continually copying other people's dress, trying to look like somebody else?

Somebody told you when you were eighteen that you looked best in shirtwaists. And that's all you've been wearing ever since.

You love orange and wear as much of it as possible—even though it makes your skin look like you're coming down with jaundice.

By most people's standards your clothes are really bizarre—unusually tight, or baggy, or loud prints and colors that scream at each other. Have you ever asked yourself why you need to draw that much attention to yourself?

In 1 Timothy 2:9 we read that "the women shall dress themselves modestly and prudently in becoming attire." Modesty is almost a forgotten word in today's society, but it is very important for the Christian woman. Today's styles don't help matters much with miniskirts, see-through blouses, and all the rest. If your skirts are so short or tight, your blouses cut too low or too tight so that a man can't help but lust when he looks at you, then you are as guilty of sin as he.

Now before you run for cover or take to the sackcloth let me say this. If a man is going to choose to lust, he will lust whether you wear modest clothing or not. A man can get turned on looking at a brick wall. But enticing clothing *can* turn a man's thoughts to lust when the last thing he wants to do is sin. Then you are as guilty as he. You aren't responsible for the thoughts he thinks when you aren't around, or when you are modestly dressed, but you *are* responsible if you encourage him to sin.

The Christian woman who wants to stay in style and still be modest may have to choose her clothes with extra care. But it isn't that difficult, really. At the height of the miniskirt craze, the more modest maxis and pantsuits were just as popular.

A single friend tells me she has a friend at work who has full permission to say, "I don't like what you're wearing. You need some new clothes. Let's go shopping," whenever she feels my friend isn't looking her best. If you aren't sure just which styles look best on you, ask the help of a friend whose taste in clothes you admire.

Whatever hairstyle, makeup, or clothing you choose, make sure they don't take up too much of your time. No man wants to wait, and wait, and wait while you apply the fourth coat of polish to your nails, glue your eyelashes in place, or tease your hair for the umpteenth time.

The Feminine You

God made men masculine and women feminine for a very special reason — because the two qualities complement each other. A normal man is attracted to a feminine woman. A normal woman is attracted to a masculine man. It's a part of God's plan that we should complement one another in this way.

"Femininity," says Helen B. Andelin in *The Fascinating Girl*, "is acquired by *accentuating the differences between yourself and men, not the similarities.* You apply this principle in your appearance, your manner, and your actions, and even your attitude. The more different you appear from men the more feminine you become."

When you choose your clothes, choose fabrics and styles that are distinctly feminine. Silk, satin, cotton, soft woolens, and synthetics are feminine. Rough woolens, denims, and tweeds are masculine. I'm not saying that everything in your wardrobe must be soft and cuddly. Even masculine fabrics and designs can be worn if the color and style are distinctly feminine. But if your wardrobe contains an overwhelming majority of masculine fabrics and styles, perhaps it's time for some new clothes.

"You acquire a feminine manner," Helen Andelin continues, "by *accentuating the differences* between yourself and men, not the similarities. Since men are strong, tough, firm, and heavy in manner, women should be delicate, tender, gentle, and light. We show this by our walk, voice, hands, and the way we carry ourselves generally."

For example, loud guffaws, slapping people on the back, and heavy footsteps are masculine. A quiet laugh, gentle pats, and walking lightly are feminine.

One of the problems of being single is that, without realizing it, you can develop just the opposite of a dependent, feminine manner. Every day you open the car door for yourself, push your way through the big glass doors at work, change light bulbs, move furniture, maybe even make minor repairs on your car. Then a man enters your life and you're suddenly supposed to be hopelessly dependent. I remember after one long, dry, no-dating spell having to actually force myself to let a man open the car door for me. I was so used to doing everything for myself I felt self-conscious having him open the door.

After one of my friends had been married about five years I asked her one day what was the secret of her obviously happy marriage. "My husband still opens the car door for me," was her reply. The mutual respect for each other's masculine and feminine qualities which was evidenced by such a simple act is beautiful to behold.

How do you treat a man's gestures toward you? Do you let him open doors for you? Seat you at the dinner table? Take your arm crossing the street?

Clean hair, well-manicured nails, polished shoes, freshly laundered and ironed clothes are attractive and feminine. Dirty or chipped nails, runover heels, pantyhose with bad snags or runs, body odors, food between the teeth, bra or slip straps that hang off your shoulder are unfeminine and unattractive.

If you feel especially defunct in social graces, why not take a charm-school course and learn how to dress and act with poise?

The Woman Men Love

The woman spoken of in Proverbs 31 is a beautiful picture of the kind of woman God would have each of us be. She is also the kind of woman to whom men are irresistibly drawn. Not one word is said about her physical features, that is, whether or not she was physically beautiful. Yet she is considered to be more valuable than precious jewels and the object of continual praise. Let's take a look at the qualities this remarkable woman possesses.

Strength of character: *Who can find a wife with strength of character? She is far more precious than jewels.*

Trustworthiness: *The heart of her husband trusts in her.*

Goodness: *She does him good and not harm all the days of her life.*

Works hard: *She . . . works with willing hands* (provides food, sews, plants a vineyard, et cetera). *She . . . eats no bread of idleness.*

Gets proper exercise: *She girds her loins with strength, and makes her arms strong.*

Business-minded: *She considers a field and buys it. She sees that her merchandise is profitable. She makes linen garments and sells them, and delivers sashes to the merchants.*

Gives to others: *She opens her palm to the poor and reaches out her hands to the needy.*

Dresses well: *She makes herself coverings, her clothing is fine linen and purple.*

Dignified: *Strength and dignity clothe her.*

Unafraid of the future: *She laughs at the future.*

Wise: *She opens her mouth with wisdom.*
Gentle: *Gentle teaching is on her tongue.*
Her family praises her: *Her children rise up and call her blessed; her husband, too, and he praises her.*

Are you attractive? Do people enjoy being around you? Attractiveness begins on the inside. The more like Christ you become, the more people will be drawn to you because they see *Him* in your life.

Maturity is not an inborn trait; it is not hereditary. It is the result of early background, environment, training, and unselfish parental love.

EDWARD A. STRECKER, M.D.

8

Cutting the Ties

You and Your Parents

Tina was an attractive woman in her early thirties when I first met her. Creative and witty, she was somewhat shy but likeable when you got to know her. But over Tina's head hung a dark cloud. She was absolutely possessed by a mother who had no intention of cutting the ties.

A very insecure woman in her own right, Tina's mother used every trick she could muster to keep Tina within her grasp. She disapproved of every man Tina dated. She forced Tina to live with her by reminding her daughter that she owed her quite a bit of money (which, unfortunately, Tina did) every time Tina tried to move out. Eventually Tina met and married a man who appreciated her good qualities, but who also realized how immature she was in many respects, thanks to her possessive mother. Some girls are not so fortunate.

Your adult years should be among the happiest in your relationship with your parents. You are an adult now and can talk with your parents on an adult level about adult interests. No longer must they scrimp and save to provide for your material needs. No longer are you dependent upon them for every decision you must make. You can sit back and enjoy each other as friends—not simply as parent and child.

74

That's the way it *should* be. But, unfortunately, in many cases the relationship between parent and child in the adult years is stormy and troubled.

When you were born, you were totally dependent upon your parents for every need—physical and emotional. You let them know when you were hungry and they fed you. You let them know when you were wet, or sick, or something hurt, and they relieved the discomfort. You giggled and cooed and they responded with ridiculous faces and nonsensical antics—and you knew they loved you. Christian educators tell us your first understanding of God consisted of the God-like qualities (or lack of same) you saw in your parents.

As you grew older, you began to discover yourself as well as your parents. You found your toes and discovered they fit nicely into your mouth. You smudged up the mirror poking fingers at the image looking back at you which you soon discovered was you. Most of your world centered around your mother since you spent most of your time with her.

Then one day you *really* discovered Daddy and your first love affair began. Mommy was competition so you pretended you didn't like her. You flirted with Daddy, giving your beginning sexual feelings a trial run, until finally you decided that maybe Mommy wasn't so bad after all and you really ought to give Daddy back to her. Especially since it was pretty obvious she had him all along.

From then on until you hit your teen or preteen years Mother and Dad could do no wrong. Then one day that wonderful dependent relationship began to change. And to everyone's dismay, you began to think that Mother and Dad could do no right! This was your way of becoming independent and standing on your own two feet. It was tough on everybody as you battled your way through your teen years. But it was necessary if you were ever going to become an independent human being.

Finally you went away to college—or to a job in the city— still wondering how your two pitiful parents could have survived so long with so little knowledge about *anything*. But as the years ticked on, you matured—and so did they (in your mind's eye at least)! Gradually you discovered that Mother and Dad weren't so dumb after all. In fact, they really knew quite a bit. This is the point at which, hopefully, you and the folks became good friends.

As your parents grow older, still another transition period will probably take place. The older they get and less able to do for themselves, the more dependent they become. To one degree or another they become the child and you become the parent. Just how pronounced this role reversal becomes depends on several things: their financial condition (must they look to you for some financial help?), their health (are they able to care for themselves?), their ability to make friends with people their own age, how much they want to be independent of their children. More and more they may begin to look to you for emotional strength when they're having problems — for someone to lean on just as you leaned on them for so many years. Suddenly you find them calling a little oftener just to see how you are, inviting you over a little oftener, asking your advice about small matters that once they would have considered too trivial to mention.

All of these stages in the parent-child relationship are normal and to be expected. It's the way God made us. But occasionally relationships develop which are not normal and which are not in God's plan for our lives. Some of these will occur whether you are married or single. Some may be uniquely the result of your unmarried state.

Between Mother and Daughter

Every normal mother wants her daughter to marry. It's a part of being a mother that nothing can take away. She wants to know that a nice man is going to "take care" of her little girl. How mature she is as an individual will determine how well she is able to accept your single state.

Some mothers never do. They push their daughters from one boy to another, desperately manipulating and maneuvering to bring about a union that will suit *them*. They are domineering and may also be possessive for a variety of reasons.

Jane was twenty-five and unmarried. And she worshiped her mother. Her mother was the "best cook," the "prettiest," the "most fun," drove the "most beautiful car." I only recall meeting Jane's mother once, but after the buildup I'd been getting it was a distinct letdown. Jane mentioned once how much her boyfriends enjoyed her mother. A friend suggested to me, "Are you sure Jane worships her mother? Sounds more like she hates her mother for competing with her." I strongly suspect my friend was correct.

Does your mother compete with you? Yes, mothers have been known to flirt with their daughters' boyfriends. Does she subtly put you down in front of your or her friends for things she imagines you do better than she?

Some mothers try to live their own lives through the lives of their daughters. They were cheated out of doing such and such when they were young, so they push their daughters into fulfilling their own private dreams. One of my mother's best friends as a child was a girl whose mother had desperately wanted to be an actress. The mother started preparing her daughter for an acting career at an early age—dancing lessons, singing lessons, the whole bit. Of course, the girl did end up being an actress, at least for a time. What choice did she have with mother pushing so hard?

Some mothers are just generally insecure (like Tina's mother) and try desperately to hold onto their daughters. Perhaps they have been the victim of an unhappy marriage, or divorce, or for other reasons have never learned to stand on their own two feet. They become masters at manipulation by inducing guilt in their daughters—"How can you think of going away for the weekend when I'm so sick I can hardly get out of my chair?" (She hasn't been truly sick since 1927.) "Where would you be if I hadn't gotten you that job?" (A lot better off.)

One of the saddest letters I ever read was a letter written to Ann Landers by a sixty-five-year-old woman who had lived all her life with a domineering, suffocating mother. Too late she realized how neurotic she was for having allowed her mother to dominate her life. Gone were her chances for marriage and a career. With only a few friends, she was left with little except a heart full of regrets for a wasted life.

If your mother is hanging onto you, Helene Arnstein, author of *Getting Along with Your Grown-up Children,* suggests that a clue to understanding why may be to look at the relationship your mother had with *her* mother. Was Gram a domineering woman who kept your mother squelched under her thumb most of the time? Maybe your mother is taking out *her* frustrations by bossing the socks off of you. If she got along well with her mother, chances are you and she will get along pretty well. If not, it's time the pattern were reversed. Reversing it is up to you.

Or maybe you're the one who's holding onto Mother. She'd have a tough time manipulating you if you weren't cooperating. Are you using your mother for a crutch? Still hiding behind her apron because you're too timid to venture forth and make a life of your own? A competent counselor can help you unravel some of the causes of an unhealthy relationship such as this.

My Heart Belongs to Daddy

Not all possessive parents are mothers. Sometimes fathers hold onto their daughters just as hard as mothers. And they, too, become masters at manipulation. Perhaps Dad's relationship with your mother was none too good. Instead of working out their differences, he simply transferred the need for companionship and affection to his daughter. How many fathers have you seen plying their daughters with expensive gifts in an attempt to win their affection?

Are you living with your father? If so, why?

"Because he needs me. Who would fix his meals, clean the house, keep him company? Daddy would be so lonely if I moved out."

Bosh! He's an adult, isn't he? Adults can usually look after themselves. Are you sure it isn't *you* who needs *him?* Most women do need a man. But a father is a father—not a substitute husband.

Is there a self-respecting man anywhere who can't provide himself with the basic necessities of life? He can learn to cook or else eat out. And I'm sure he's capable of operating a washing machine at the local laundromat. If he is the kind who won't get out and make friends, that's *his* problem. Don't make it yours. If he can't afford a housekeeper, offer to come over occasionally and bail things out for him. Invite him over to dinner now and then. But don't allow him to manipulate you into devoting your life to caring for dear old Dad. Dad can take care of himself.

Now I'm not saying that an adult woman should never live with her parents. Obviously, there are always exceptions to the rule. But from my observations, most single women who live with their parents do so because they have never quite grown up. An important part of maturity is making a life for yourself— standing on your own two feet.

You say you want to get married? Suppose some nice man does get his foot in the door between you and Mother. "Know thy mother-in-law" was my husband's rule of thumb when we were preparing to marry. How eager is that man going to be to sweep you off your feet when it's obvious to everyone that Mother holds the broom. If she's telling you what to do now—and you're letting her—he knows good and well the situation isn't likely to change after you get married.

The Bible teaches that we are to respect and honor our parents. That does not mean we are to let them rule our lives. A man is to "leave his father and mother and cling to his wife." (I'm sure that applies to women as well.) In the face of oriental customs, that may seem like a curious command. When a man married, he usually did not leave his parents' home. Instead, a section for him and his bride was added onto the family tent! The meaning, therefore, must involve more than physical separation from one's parents. Obviously, it refers to emotional independence. If the individual is old enough to marry, the ties must be cut between parent and child.

Some parents do not want to cut those ties—or don't know how. But for each of us to develop into mature Christian women the ties must be cut. You may be the one who has to do it.

Test Yourself

If you are living with one or both of your parents (and you are past college age), ask yourself a few questions.

1. With whom do you spend your vacations? Mom? Dad? Alone? A friend?

2. When you entertain guests or are invited out, are either of your parents usually present?

3. Do your parents ever say things to you like: "Who was that on the telephone?" "What time did you get home last night?" "I wish you wouldn't date so-and-so. I don't like him." "Why do you want to go bowling with Sue tonight? I thought we'd barbecue steaks here at home. I bought fillets because I know how much you like them."

4. Whenever you try to make plans (vacation, social engagements, et cetera), does your mother (or father) always have an alternate plan that involves just the two of you?

5. What kind of life would you have if your parents passed away tomorrow?

It is God's purpose out of evil
still to bring forth good.
AUTHOR UNKNOWN

9

Lost — and Found

The Widowed and Divorced

She turned away from the fresh grave. Only by forcing herself was she able to move one foot ahead of the other, taking the steps that would lead her away. Away from him . . . forever.

She felt the others watching her. They were nice, but how could they possibly understand? Could they know what grief it was to lose your husband . . . your *young* husband? She had often wondered if she would be able to bear it when they were old and gray, but she had never thought — never guessed — that it might happen like this. Then, the unthinkable had happened, and there was no time to prepare. Really, it wasn't as if something had happened, so much as it was that everything had *ceased* to happen. Everything for her, at least. For *he* had ceased to be, and only the mound of dirt would prove that he had been. And where was he now . . .?

"No, no, you must not think; not *that,* anyway." One part of her mind had taken over, mercifully, and was directing her to action. . . . Concentrate on what you are doing. Bend down. Scoop up dirt. (The others each had a handful of dirt.) Fling it on the grave. (The others had flung theirs on the mound, as they passed by, in customary ritual.) Now, throw the dirt. (The ritual goes on, and *life* goes on . . . somewhere.) But she could not throw the dirt. It sifted to the ground through her limp fingers, and she turned away.

Where to go now? What to do? Go home? Stay with her husband's people until the shock passed? All of a sudden she knew only that it mattered terribly that no one touch her right hand; some of the dirt was still clinging to it.

In the future the shock would pass, but not the hurt. In the future she would have a decision to make, and would choose to go God's way, to the best of her knowledge. There would be surprises and even joy; but now there was just hurt.

How could she know that at that very moment a godly man was busy prospering his business, and would one day share his wealth with her as her God-given husband? How could she know that she would be blessed with children and children's children? That throughout the world her name would become a symbol of purity and devoted love and would be given fondly to many daughters? Or, most astounding of all, that she would be one of the only two Gentiles in the distinguished line of the Messiah?

Ruth—an ancestor of Christ because her husband died and she later married a Jew named Boaz.

"For now we see through a glass, darkly; but then face to face...."

                                                    MARTHA CHRISTINE WHITE

When Death Takes a Husband

Some of you reading this book have lost your husband through death. Perhaps you had warning. Perhaps you did not. One of my dearest friends awoke one morning to find her husband dying beside her. No illness. No warning. And to this day there has been no medical explanation for his death.

Watching someone you love suffer with an incurable illness is perhaps the hardest thing we have to face in this life. Losing a husband without any warning is also hard. Nothing anyone can say or do eases the pain in your heart.

Your first reaction, no doubt, was, Why? Why did this happen to me? Why would God allow such a tragedy to occur? What purpose could such a loss possibly serve? Such thoughts are normal but they dare not remain in your thinking for long. I'm sure Ruth had her moments of wondering why God permitted the death of her husband. But that was because she could not see ahead to the blessings God had for her in the future.

None of us can escape sorrow. At some time in our lives all of us will lose someone dear to us. The important thing is that God can take those seeming tragedies and make of them something good—if we will only let Him. Death is the result of the sin that entered the world back in the Garden of Eden. But "it is God's

purpose out of evil still to bring forth good," I once heard someone say. [The more you are able to commit your heartache to Him,
the more opportunity you give Him to use your loss for His
honor and glory.]

"I'm *lost* without him," Ruth no doubt mourned when her first
husband died. But before long she *found* herself in the loving
care of God.

The Divorced Woman

Some of you reading this book are divorced. After ten years
with an alcoholic husband you couldn't hack it any longer and
filed for divorce. After five years of marriage he decided he was
in love with another woman and *he* checked out. After one year
of marriage you discovered you were hopelessly mismatched and
had the marriage annulled. Whatever the reason, you now find
yourself one of the statistics — a victim of divorce.

Divorce is especially hard for a Christian woman because the
Bible is so explicit about the permanence of marriage. Many
Christians don't know quite what to do with the divorcée, and
many divorcées don't really know what to do with themselves.

Some Christians heap burdens upon the divorced person that
God never intended them to have. Nowhere in Scripture does
God say that divorce is the unpardonable sin. Yet divorcées in
some Christian circles are treated as if it were. When I was growing up a divorced person was not even allowed to teach a Sunday-
school class.

I am not in favor of divorce and I cannot excuse the person who
willfully marries outside of God's will or deliberately creates
situations that produce divorce. But because of man's sinful
nature, I am forced to recognize that in some situations, short of a
miracle, divorce is inevitable. People make mistakes in their
choice of a marriage partner just as surely as they flunk exams in
college or push the wrong button on a computer. Growth and
maturity take time and some people mature more slowly than
others. The very circumstances that broke up your marriage,
however, can be used by God to help mature you and draw you
close to Him. God's love and forgiveness are there for the taking.

One of the dearest Christian women I ever met told me that when her marriage broke up her entire world collapsed. During the mental and physical collapse that resulted she totally committed herself to God. When I knew her, many years after her divorce, she was a delightful Christian woman serving faithfully in the church. So far as I know she still is. It was actually because of her divorce that she found Christ.

One of the biggest problems for the Christian divorcée centers around the matter of remarriage. Few of us relish the thought of facing the rest of our lives alone. Yet the Bible has some very important teachings about divorce and remarriage that cannot be ignored.

Let me make one thing clear at this point. I am not going to tell you whether or not I think you can or cannot remarry. There are about as many interpretations of the passages relating to divorce and remarriage as there are people to provide interpretations. If you have not reached a decision regarding remarriage, running from one minister to another or from one Bible commentary to another will do you little good. In fact it will probably only serve to confuse you the more. One person says you can remarry and another person says you can't. With a minimum of effort you can easily stack the evidence whichever way you want it to go.

Like every decision in the Christian life, your decision to remarry or not to remarry must be strictly your own. Read everything the Bible has to say about the subject and talk it over with God until He shows you clearly His will for your life. Don't rush into anything. Be honest with yourself and with God about your feelings in the matter. Only through complete honesty and a willingness to do His will can you ever hope to discover His perfect will for your life.

There are some things concerning divorce about which the Bible is pretty specific. For the sake of those of you who are not yet married, as well as those who are divorced, let's take a look at the Book.

1. God's original and perfect plan is for two people to marry and stay married. " '. . . therefore shall a man leave his father

and mother (and shall cling to his wife) and the two shall be one flesh'; so that they are no longer two, but one flesh. What God, therefore, has joined, let not man divide" (Mark 10:7-9).

2. Moses permitted divorce because of the hardness of men's hearts, but this was not part of God's perfect plan (see Mark 10:2-6).

3. Jesus permitted divorce for one reason only: unfaithfulness. "But I tell you that anyone who divorces his wife, except for unfaithfulness, makes her commit adultery . . ." (Matthew 5:32).

4. Paul, under the inspiration of the Holy Spirit, but not under direct command from Christ, permits divorce as a result of desertion. "So, if the wife has a nonbelieving husband who enjoys living with her, let her not divorce her husband. . . . In case the nonbeliever wants to separate, let there be separation; the brother or sister is under such circumstances not tied down. But God has called you to enjoy peace" (1 Corinthians 7:13, 15).

From my understanding of Scripture, I do not find any conditions that permit remarriage for the divorced person, with the possible exception of unfaithfulness and desertion. To remarry under any other conditions is to commit adultery. However, even if circumstances do permit you to remarry, some people should not remarry for other reasons.

Too many people enter marriage with the idea that if things don't work out they can always get a divorce and start over. The more relaxed our divorce laws become the easier it is for people to slip in and out of marriage. If you marry too young or without careful thought, the chances of a successful marriage are exceedingly slim. A marriage contract with an "easy out" clause was never part of God's plan.

The best time to prevent divorce is before you get married. After marriage it may be too late. In the last chapter of this book we'll talk about some of the ways you can make your marriage secure before you ever take those vows.

As bad as divorce is, however, it is not the end of the world. Remember the twelve tribes of Israel? One tribe, the Levites, was singled out by God to be the priests. "But Moses did not grant a heritage to the tribe of Levi, because, as he told them, the Lord God of Israel is their heritage" (Joshua 13:33).

One would think that the Levites must have been especially holy in order to be chosen for such lofty service. But a tragic story precedes their selection. Genesis 34:25–31 tells us that two brothers, Simeon and Levi, were involved in murder and were rebuked for their evil deed by their father, Jacob. Both were cursed for their wickedness, but Levi saw that curse turned into a blessing.

As Alan Redpath explains it in *Victorious Christian Living:*

> There was nothing in the early years of Simeon and Levi which indicated God's future purpose. Their early life was shameful; they had brought disgrace on themselves, on their tribe, and on their families. But, my friends, is it not true that God restores the years that the cankerworm has eaten? Does He not take soiled hearts and cleanse them? Does He not take clay that has been marred in the hands of the potter and make it again another vessel? Yes, indeed He does! *Never does our God allow past history, however unpleasant or however sinful, to prevent Him from allotting to us a unique place in His service* [italics mine].

Why were the Levites chosen for service in spite of their past? Look at Exodus 32:26 for the answer. Standing before the people Moses cried out, "Who is on the Lord's side? let him come unto me" (KJV). Every Levite to a man responded to the call, repented of his sin, and turned to God. The curse that had been pronounced on Simeon eventually ran its course and the entire tribe faded out of existence. Levi and his tribe, however, had their curse turned into a blessing through repentance.

Have you allowed God to turn the curse of your divorce into a blessing? Have you repented of your part in whatever caused the divorce? (It will do no good to try and place all the blame on your ex-husband.) Have you asked God to free you from any bitterness or resentment? Have you asked Him to help you correct any faults of yours that may have contributed to the divorce? Redpath writes, in the same book:

To imagine . . . that a person who entered into a marriage that has proved disastrous must carry all through his life the stigma of it, is to place a burden on him which is utterly contrary to the Book and which the grace of Christ can utterly remove.

Thank God that in the moment when someone has been crushed seemingly beyond help, when the things that he has cherished most in life have crashed around him, and he is left in the shattered wreck of what once he thought was a home, the Lord Jesus holds out His hand to aid. Thank God, He takes the clay that has been marred, the precious, soiled, broken life, and molds it again, now into a vessel unto honor, sanctified, and meet for the Master's use. And He says, "From this moment onward the Lord thy God is thy inheritance."

Has God become your inheritance? Have you found the special place of service God has for you?

At times you ought to stay alone
I make so bold as to advise
And just be friendly with your
   soul—
Your soul will miss you otherwise.

REBECCA MC CANN

10

Alone — or Lonely

What to Do When You've Got the "Poor Mes"

It had been one of those days for my husband. A rat race at work. Running here and there. People. Telephones. Questions. Answers. It was late at night before things began to settle down. Not really realizing how weary he was, I was about to make some additional demand on his time when he stopped me short.

"I haven't been alone all day," he said, looking almost as harried as he felt.

About the greatest fun we have is just being together. Yet as married people we realize the importance of each of us being alone at times. I'm home alone during the day. My husband isn't. So I usually try to allow some time in the evening for him to be alone if he wants to. We needed time alone when we were single. We need it now, too.

The single years afford much more opportunity to be alone than you'll ever have when you get married and have children. Some girls enjoy being alone. Others dread it. But the ability to be happily alone is one of the healthiest qualities you can cultivate.

To be alone means simply that you are all by yourself. It is a physical thing. Loneliness, on the other hand, is psychological. The lonely person may be surrounded with people, but he feels like he is the only person in the world. "Loneliness," says William E. Park in *The Quest for Inner Peace*, "is when you are forced to be alone against your will; solitude is when, like Thoreau, you are willingly alone." Aloneness is positive. Loneliness is negative.

Consider for a moment some of the values of spending time alone. Sometimes you need to be alone just so you can catch up with yourself. If you've been burning the candle at both ends, stay home one night for a change. Turn on some soft music, take a leisurely bath, and hit the sack early. Rest and relaxation are an important part of staying healthy. Isaiah 30:15 (KJV) says that "in quietness and in confidence shall be your strength." Sometimes you can best achieve that strength when you are alone.

Just as your body needs rest and restoration, so does your mind. The psalmist said, "He leads me beside restful water; He revives my soul," (Psalms 23:3). Restoration of the soul takes place beside the restful waters, not in the hustle and bustle of activity. Creative use of your time alone provides the physical and mental strength you need to cope with the problems that face us all from day to day.

Where you spend your time alone is up to you. But it's interesting to note that the psalmist mentions the restfulness of water. How many times have you paused to watch a tumbling waterfall, felt the cool spray from a fountain, or studied your reflection in a shimmering pond—and wished you didn't have to leave? Some of my most restful moments have been listening to the waves lap against the shore at the ocean. I wouldn't dare live overlooking the ocean. The waves would mesmerize me in no time and I'd never get anything done. If you're feeling extra tired, don't overlook the possibility of a weekend spent relaxing at a lake or the seashore.

Another value of spending time alone is the opportunity it affords us to find direction for our lives. Why are we here? What are we doing? Where are we going? These are important questions that each of us must answer if we are going to lead meaningful lives. Like the man who jumped on his horse and rode off in all directions, our lives sometimes become a mumbo jumbo of activity until we wonder if we're accomplishing anything at all. We try first one thing, then another, never satisfied with anything. The problem, perhaps, is that we've never spent time alone with ourselves thinking through what life is all about.

The only way you can truly find direction for your life, of course, is to spend time alone with God. As surely as He allowed you to be born He has a plan for your life. He sent His Son to die that you might live. He provided a written Word to guide you step by step. He sent His Holy Spirit to comfort you and help you live God's way. But none of what God has provided will ever be a reality for you until you spend time alone with Him. Not time spent telling Him all your troubles. (Of course, He wants you to do that, too. He's called the Comforter for a reason.) But you must also spend time listening to Him speak to you. That's not something you do at a moment's notice. It takes time— alone.

Being alone also provides opportunity for you to develop your creativity. It isn't likely that the great music of Mozart or the poetry of Keats was written in the middle of a crowded room. I have an author friend who can write a book sitting in the living room of his home with a typewriter on his lap and the children playing nearby. But he's a rare one. Most of us need peace and quiet before the ideas start to come. You think you aren't creative? Maybe that's because you've never spent time alone to find out.

"But I'm So Lonely"

No matter how creatively we may use our time alone, however, there will be times when all of us feel lonely. Perhaps you have lost your husband through death or divorce, or recently broken an engagement to someone you truly loved. Until you are over the shock of separation, you will undoubtedly have periods of loneliness. Or perhaps you miss a special friend who is away, or wish you had a man. Occasional lonely moments are normal and inevitable. If we didn't *care* about people we wouldn't be lonely.

In the questionnaire about the single life which I used as research for this book, I asked the single women to complete three sentences with the first words that came to mind: "Loneliness is . . . ." "I feel lonely . . . ." and "I feel lonely especially when . . . ." Some of the girls defined loneliness as follows. Do you agree with their definitions?

Loneliness is:
> self-centeredness.
> pity for oneself.
> inability to receive and give.
> not having a special someone to share with.
> wanting to be with someone and being alone.
> not knowing Christ as your Saviour.
> isolation from loved ones.
> a state of feeling regardless of who is around you.
> being and feeling unwanted.
> when you feel less important than the smallest star.
> an empty feeling.
> feeling sorry for yourself.
> being alone in a big city where you don't know a soul.
> needing people but afraid to call anyone for fear of being rebuffed.
> needing someone to need you.
> not being able to share yourself and your thoughts with someone who cares.

Instead of *defining* loneliness, some girls *reacted* to it. Have you ever felt the way they feel?

Do you feel that loneliness is:
> my own fault.
> the lot of the single person.
> my middle name.
> unhealthy.

all around me.
depressing.
bearable but unpleasant.
probably the biggest thing single people fear.
frightening at times.

Or do you see loneliness as:
a battle but not limited to the single.
easily overcome if we would seek Jesus' face.
healthy sometimes—what I do with it is especially important.
miserable but perhaps makes you more appreciative of others.
beneficial when it enables one to be creative in his loneliness or as a result of the experience of loneliness.
different from being alone. Sometimes I like to be alone.
not a bad feeling—reminds one to turn to the Lord.
helpful in drawing closer to God.
the worst feeling one can have, but it can lead to spiritual growth and personal insight.

For some people loneliness is a chronic problem. They are haunted by the feeling that nobody loves them, nobody cares.

Some people feel lonely because they do not have any close friends. They lack the social skills necessary to develop meaningful relationships with people and have no one to whom they can truly open up their hearts.

How close are you and your best friend? Are there people—both men and women—in whom you feel free to confide? Is there anyone whose shoulder you can literally cry on if you feel like it? If making friends is a problem for you, a competent counselor can help you discover what is preventing you from sharing yourself with others.

Look back at the definitions for loneliness listed earlier. Which of those definitions best sums up the basic cause of loneliness? If you chose "self-centeredness" you are quite right. Prolonged loneliness is the result of feeling sorry for yourself, self-pity—in short, a preoccupation with yourself. Without realizing it your innermost self may be saying, "Poor me. I've got nobody and nothing. If somebody else won't give me some attention I'll give it to myself. Poor, poor me." Or maybe you drag your "poor mes" with you wherever you go—using them as a device to get attention and sympathy. It may work for awhile, but eventually people get tired of listening to other people's sob stories. Instead of getting attention, you may find people turning their backs on you altogether.

The woman who gives of herself to others has little time to feel lonely. The love that she gives to others is returned in abundance. Maybe your problem is that you aren't involved enough in service to other people.

The danger with prolonged loneliness is that it tends to lead to things that are worse. The pattern goes something like this.

You feel lonely. You wish you had a man. And so you think, *If only I had a man I wouldn't be lonely.*

The more you think about it the more depressed you become. The more depressed you become the angrier you get.

Why don't *I have a man? Doesn't God like me? Why is He denying me the very thing I need most?*

Or maybe you get mad at yourself.

If I weren't so ugly (tall, short, fat, thin, stupid, intelligent) I would *have a man. Nobody wants a dumb cluck like me.*

The anger at yourself, others, or God leads finally to guilt. because you've always been taught that a Christian isn't supposed to get angry. And so the vicious circle continues.

Loneliness leads to depression which leads to anger which leads to guilt. No matter where you begin on the circle, one thing leads to another. Anger and unhappiness that were smoldering underneath suddenly ignite. The pattern is set and unless you take steps to correct it, it will develop into a life-style that lasts for years — perhaps all of your life.

What to Do When You've Got the "Poor Mes"

How can you overcome loneliness?

The first step is to put loneliness in its proper perspective. Nobody has a corner on loneliness, least of all you. Single people are lonely at times. So are married people. When you stop to think about it, what could be more lonely than living in the same house with someone who no longer loves you or someone you no longer love?

Listed below are some of the times when single girls say they are most apt to feel lonely. As you read through the list, check those which apply primarily to single women, those which apply to married women, and those which are a particular problem for you.

I feel lonely when:	Single Women	Married Women	Me
I have nothing to do.	_____	_____	___
I am by myself too long.	_____	_____	___
my friends are getting married.	_____	_____	___
I'm around a lot of couples by myself.	_____	_____	___
it's my birthday or a special holiday and I don't have a "special" man to share it with.	_____	_____	___
I am not loved.	_____	_____	___
I go shopping.	_____	_____	___
I have my period which makes me more aware of my desire for marriage and children.	_____	_____	___
I feel I have let someone down.	_____	_____	___
others are dating and I'm not.	_____	_____	___

	Single Women	Married Women	Me
I'm physically tired.	_____	_____	___
I've come close to dating the special guy and the date has fallen through.	_____	_____	___
I see others enjoying family life.	_____	_____	___
I'm with a group of couples and I'm the only single on the weekends.	_____	_____	___
viewing a beautiful scene alone.	_____	_____	___
I am selfish.	_____	_____	___
I think about the past and future.	_____	_____	___
I have decisions to make.	_____	_____	___
I can't be with men at least several times a week (married or not).	_____	_____	___
I have a disagreement with someone.	_____	_____	___
I am discouraged.	_____	_____	___
I'm with people with whom I'm not at ease.	_____	_____	___
plans for a date fall through.	_____	_____	___
I don't have a guy around that I care for.	_____	_____	___
I feel that I have failed in some important task.	_____	_____	___
I think of men I admire.	_____	_____	___
my roommate has a date or my friends have a date.	_____	_____	___
I think about the man I once loved.	_____	_____	___
in a crowd.	_____	_____	___
it's nighttime.	_____	_____	___
I sit around and think about it.	_____	_____	___
I can't see the reasons for what God is doing for me.	_____	_____	___

Be honest about your emotions. If you feel lonely or angry
or scared, admit it. Only then can you deal with it constructively.

At the root of chronic loneliness is the feeling that nobody
cares. But all you have to do is pick up your Bible to realize that
Somebody *does* care. Jesus said, ". . . lo, I am with you alway,
even unto the end of the world" (Matthew 28:20 kjv). The writer
of Hebrews 13:5 (kjv) reminds us that God has said, "I will never
leave thee, nor forsake thee." In John 15:13, 14 Jesus said, "No
one has greater love than this: to lay down his life for his friends.
You are My friends if you do what I command you."

At first glance, saying that God is with you when you're lonely
may seem a little impractical when what you really want is a
warm body next to yours. But if there isn't a warm body next to
yours, you'd better get acquainted with whatever is in second
place. And through the experience you just might discover that
second place is better than first. God never lets you down. God
is always with you. God loves you—no matter what. God wants
to give you only what is best for you. God's best gifts bring joy.
God's shoulder is always ready for you to cry on. Now wherever
could you find a better friend than that? Commit your loneliness
to God and ask Him to remove it or use it for His glory.

Some situations that produce loneliness are predictable. Be
prepared for them.

If you always drag bottom on Friday nights when you don't
have a date, plan something exciting for the weekend. Don't
resign yourself to a lonely evening at home.

If physical weariness or the beginning of your menstrual
period are sure to produce a case of the "poor mes," recognize
it for what it is. When the pangs of loneliness hit, remind yourself
that the cause is largely physical and will go away of its own
accord in a few hours or days.

Holidays are often difficult because they are usually family-
centered. And if you are away from your family you feel left out
and alone. If a family whose friendship you enjoy invites you for
the holidays, go and be your cheeriest self. Sometimes, however,
people make you feel worse instead of better. I'll never forget

the well-meaning lady at church who once invited me to Thanksgiving dinner and informed me that she was trying to round up
the "strays" (or words to that effect) who had nowhere else to go.
I made up my mind I would definitely have someplace else to go.

Another year I decided to become the master of my own fate.
Instead of counting myself among the rejects, I invited a family
to have Thanksgiving dinner with me at my apartment. Their
oldest son had just entered the service and I thought *they* might
be a little lonely without him. It was one of the happiest holidays
I ever spent.

One of the definitions of loneliness listed earlier in this
chapter was "needing people but afraid to call anyone for fear of
being rebuffed." A friend tells me this was not a problem for
her when she lived with someone, but became a problem when
she lived alone. For example, she might want to call a girl friend
and ask if they could have dinner together, but she was afraid of
being turned down. So she protected herself by planning alternate activities that she would also enjoy. At the top of the list
would be having dinner with her friend. But if the friend had
other plans, there were a couple of other activities she could fall
back on and enjoy.

Look back at the situations you've checked which are most apt
to make you feel lonely. How many of those can you predict and
plan for in advance?

While many situations are predictable, some are not. No
matter how popular you may be, sooner or later you end up with
an unplanned evening at home. A big date fell through at the last
minute, your plans for a ski weekend ran amuck, or your car
broke down on the way out of town, and you're stuck at home.
Unless you have some inner resources to draw upon, such times
can be disastrous.

If loneliness is about to set in, work five minutes at something
— sewing, cleaning house, trying a new recipe — and it will
usually get you over the hump. When asked what she does on
Friday night, one girl replied, "Sometimes I cry and then I clean
out my dresser drawers." At other times she loses herself in a
good book and enjoys the evening alone. (By the way, there's

nothing wrong with having a good cry once in awhile. It may be just what you need to clear out the emotional cobwebs.)

The wider your interests the less chance you have to get lonely. Do you have any hobbies? Are you reasonably proficient at at least one sport? Now is a good time to develop some hobbies, learn a new language, improve your skills at sports, or volunteer your services at the church or some other service organization. Here are the ways some single women tell me they spend their free time when they don't have a date:

    volunteer hospital work
    sponsor a youth group
    organize, plan, and attend group social activities, Bible studies,
        prayer groups, dinner parties
    refinish furniture
    attend our single adult functions
    go to Christian socials that are on Friday and/or Saturday
        nights
    read the Bible (Do you have a plan for studying the Bible?
        Check with your local Christian bookstore for some books
        on how to study the Bible. Or take a course at a Christian
        college or Bible school. You can get hooked studying the
        Bible and the time will fly.)
    play golf alone
    go stag to school banquets and church affairs (Now there's a
        brave girl!)
    go bowling
    stay home and sew
    catch up on needed sleep
    help with church work where there are men involved
I belong to a lodge and a professional organization.

The possibilities are endless, limited only by your own imagination.

My final suggestion is that you make your loneliness work for you. For example, you attend a party and there isn't a soul there you know. You feel terribly lonely. The next time you attend a party where you *do* know the people, think about that poor girl over in the corner who is alone and trying desperately to look like she isn't. What can you do to make her feel less lonely?

Whatever makes you lonely undoubtedly makes someone else lonely, too. Your girl friend may be as lonely as you on a dateless evening and unendingly grateful for a telephone call or an invitation to come over and watch TV or sew. Use the lonely times to heighten your sensitivity to the loneliness of others.

Do You Really Like Yourself?

The more mature we become the better use we are able to make of our moments alone. The essence of healthy aloneness, of course, is self-love. Not in any selfish sense. But in the sense of — do you like yourself? Do you feel comfortable with yourself? Can you entertain yourself, keep yourself company? Or does someone else have to entertain you? Are you your own best friend? If you don't like yourself, it stands to reason you won't enjoy being alone with yourself.

The second greatest commandment given by Jesus was to love your neighbor *as you love yourself* (*see* Matthew 22:39). In his *Commentary on the Whole Bible,* Matthew Henry tells us, "There is a self-love which is corrupt, and the root of the greatest sins, and it must be put off and mortified: but there is a self-love which is natural, and the rule of the greatest duty, and it must be preserved and sanctified. We must love ourselves, that is, we must have a due regard to the dignity of our own natures, and a due concern for the welfare of our own souls and bodies."

You cannot be a true friend to someone else until you are on friendly terms with yourself. You cannot accept someone else until you accept yourself. You cannot truly love someone else until you first love God and then yourself.

Check Up on Yourself

What do you do when you don't have a date?

    ____I usually stay home and enjoy it.

    ____I call up a girl friend and we go somewhere.

    ____I go visit someone.

    ____I usually just stay home depressed.

    ____Other:_____._____

When are you most likely to feel lonely? What can you do to prevent loneliness from overpowering you at those times?

Do you regularly feel depressed?

Do you really like yourself? If not, why not?

Like one girl, are you lonely "more of the time than I acknowledge to myself or God"?

Read Psalms 17:8 (KJV). Have you ever felt like you were the apple of God's eye?

Only God could create something as beautiful as sex. Only Satan could make it so ugly.

11

On Saintliness and Sex

Is It the Holy Spirit or Hormones?

It all started when God looked at Adam and declared in those historic words, "It is not good for the man to be alone" (Genesis 2:18). And so He created someone very special to keep Adam company. A human being who was similar to Adam, but just different enough to make life interesting. He made for Adam a woman.

As part of His creation, God placed in Adam a physical desire toward Eve and the same kind of desire in Eve toward Adam. He gave them eyes so they could see each other. He gave them a sense of touch so they could feel the warmth of each other's bodies. He gave them a sense of smell so that Adam could smell the subtle fragrance of that flower tucked behind Eve's ear. He gave them ears so they could hear each other's whispered words of love. Just as God had evaluated the other aspects of His creation, He looked at Adam and Eve and pronounced them "good."

Later on, the physical desire God had given them bore fruit— and the first human babies were born into the world. Had there been no physical desire the human race would have begun and ended in the Garden of Eden.

But before any children were born, along came Satan. And the perfect beauty of sex has been tarnished ever since.

Sex is one of the most beautiful aspects of God's creation. It is the ultimate physical expression of love between two people—

a degree of intimacy that was designed by God to help bind two people together in a marriage relationship. "Only God could create something as beautiful as sex," I once heard my mother say, "and only Satan could make it so ugly." Sex in the proper context adds beauty to life. The improper use of sex dissipates and destroys.

Our bodies and the sex drive with which we are equipped are a normal, healthy part of God's creation. There is no reason why you should ever be ashamed of any of it. To be ashamed of any part of your body is to say in essence, "God, you made a mistake." To be ashamed of your sexual feelings is to deny one of the beautiful purposes of being a woman—the ability to give yourself to a man in love and to bear children.

In today's society, however, more girls seem ready to take *off* their clothes than to hide their bodies in shame. In this day of permissiveness, anything goes, and it usually goes—*off.* Clothes, inhibitions, and morals. In a society that denies any Absolute Authority, we are told to become our own authorities. Set your own standards. Determine your own code of ethics. Put together your own moral guidelines. And whatever you come up with is right.

As Christians, it is easy to acknowledge with our intellects that such a philosophy is wrong. But when it comes right down to the practical application of it all, some Christian girls end up in confusion and despair.

To understand the role of sex in our lives and in society, there are a few facts we need to keep in mind.

• Sex is an important physical drive, but it is only one of several such drives. How about the hunger drive, the need for water to sustain life, the need for sleep? Which drive affects you the most often—the need for food, or the need to satisfy your sexual appetite? Assuming you haven't yet given up three meals a day, which of these drives is really the most important?

• Sex is the one physical drive we *can* live without. You can't live without food or water or rest or air. But you can live a happy, useful, successful life without sex.

• Sex is powerful and like any powerful force it must be controlled and channeled constructively. An uncontrolled appetite for food results in obesity. An uncontrolled appetite for sex leads to immorality and heartache.

• All this talk about sexual liberation is about as new as mashed potatoes. To hear some exponents of the "new" morality, you'd think permissiveness was invented in the twentieth century. In point of fact, however, the moral values in any given period of time have always included everything from Victorian prudery to permissiveness. The city of Sodom, you may recall, was so full of homosexuals God had to evict Lot and destroy the entire "liberated" city.

The "new" morality is as old as man. Thanks to mass communication, people *talk* about sex a lot more than they used to. But man has been practicing sex in its moral and immoral forms since time began.

• *Normal sex* is the physical union which takes place between husband and wife within the bonds of marriage. Any deviation from that norm is contrary to Scripture, a violation of the beauties of God's creation, and will inevitably lead to heartbreak. Sex outside of marriage and abnormal sex are just plain sin.

Satan is no dummy. He recognizes our permissive society for what it is — an opportunity for him to capture men's (and women's) souls. And his methods of temptation are numerous.

He tempts us *visually* — through billboards, magazines, books, newspapers, movies, TV. *Playboy* magazine wasn't enough. Now we have similar sex-oriented magazines designed especially for women. Forget that nonsense about such magazines having "redeeming social value." Their purpose is to tempt and entice you to sin.

He tempts us *verbally*. Your boyfriend says, "If you really love me . . . ." A well-known psychiatrist says, *"Any Woman Can!"*

He tempts us through *familiarity*. We live in a world so outspoken about sex that after awhile familiarity breeds acceptance. Black looks more like white. Immorality seems much more moral. We begin to doubt our own judgments.

He tempts us through the *opinions of "respected" people*. A marriage counselor friend tells me he recently examined a book on sex technique which is currently on the best-seller list. Complete with color photographs, it was edited by a man who boasts a Ph.D. "When I was in high school," my friend commented, "such a book would have been considered pornography." Recently I heard a well-known comedian on TV joking about a situation that bordered on bestiality.

He tempts us through *our own thought life*. Sometimes he is direct. Sometimes he is subtle. Always he aims at our weakest point. "Sometimes I think," writes a Christian woman fighting the chains of lesbianism, "why not just go into it all the way? Then you'll find out how awful that kind of life really is and you won't want to do it anymore." Fortunately, she recognized that thought for the satanic attack that it is.

He tempts us through *availability*. Those sexy magazines and books are right out there on the newsstand for you to look at—not hidden underneath the cash register. Nobody is going to stop you from going to an X-rated movie if you really want to. Birth-control devices are available at the drugstore. It's hard to turn your back on something that stares you in the face every time you turn around.

Just as sure as there is a Satan to tempt us, however, there is a God to save us from that temptation. And that God has stated it very plainly.

> No temptation beyond human resistance has laid hold on you, and God is reliable, who will not permit you to be tempted beyond your ability, but will at the time of temptation provide a way out, so that you will be able to stand it.
>
> 1 Corinthians 10:13

The important thing for you to do is to discover that "way out."

Premarital Sex

Being a virgin isn't easy. Especially in this day and age. If you listen to Helen Gurley Brown and her followers, you are bombarded with suggestions that a woman isn't really a woman until she's gone to bed with a man. Seems like the only person who wants you to remain a virgin these days is your mother.

Why should you be a virgin? In this day of "enlightenment," "freedom," and the Pill, why should you wait for sexual fulfillment until marriage? Let's look at some of the reasons.

How many *firsts* can you remember in your life? Your first frilly party dress. Your first bicycle. Your first date. Whether the event was large or small, some firsts stand out in our memories because they were especially enjoyable (or unpleasant) and because it was the first time we had encountered that situation.

The first time you have intercourse with a man, something happens inside you. You are never the same person after that. That event was meant by God to take place between you and the man you love and respect within the bonds of marriage. In that setting it is beautiful and sacred. An event never to be forgotten. No other sexual experience will be the same as the first time the man you love demonstrates his love by entering your body with his.

Contrary to the attitude expressed by many people today, sex is not a commodity to be bought or sold—or even given—at random. Sex is *you*, not an object you take out of a drawer now and then when you want to have a little fun. When you give your body to a man, you are giving *yourself*. Don't ever think you can divorce the two. It just doesn't work.

In order for sex to be the beautiful experience it was meant to be several conditions must be met. The experience must be *free of guilt*. No matter how much you may try to convince yourself otherwise, sex outside of marriage will leave you with feelings of guilt.

The experience must also be *accompanied by security*. Sex is a private affair between husband and wife with nobody looking on. It also requires the security of marriage. Why? Well, for one reason, not all first experiences (or second or third or even fourth) are all that great. In fact, for some women the experience is rather painful in the beginning. As husband and wife you will work this out and learn together within the permanent arrangement called marriage. A "hit and run" affair between two unmarried people can leave deep emotional scars. There is no security in a guilty conscience.

Many men can go from one affair to another with no thoughts of marriage. A woman can't. Down deep inside a normal woman will be the thought, "Surely he'll marry me eventually." What if he does? Do you want to marry a man who plays around before he gets married? What assurance do you have that he won't play around after he is married? And if he doesn't marry you, could it be because he doesn't trust *your* loyalty after marriage either?

The laws of God are not to be tampered with and the Bible strictly forbids both fornication (sex before marriage) and adultery. God's laws were given in love because He cares about us and knows what is best for us. Since He created sex it stands to reason that He understands even better than we do why it can never be satisfying outside of marriage.

Suppose you have played around already. Is it too late to make a new start? Certainly not. The God who established laws against illicit sex also established the law of forgiveness. No sin is too great to be forgiven. When you come to God in repentance He is more than willing to forgive—and forget. Commit the matter to Him and leave it there. If God wants you to marry, He will send along a man who will love and accept you, despite the mistakes of the past.

Faith and Frustration

Okay, so you've convinced yourself that you're going to wait until marriage. But when all is said and done, the sex drive is still there, isn't it? You're going to feel the same way next month right before or after your period, aren't you? So what can you do about it?

Know when the desire is likely to hit the hardest and be prepared for it. Are your sexual feelings the strongest before, after or during your period? Do you feel depressed? Crabby? Domestic? Nervous? If being around men helps calm your nerves, plan activities that include men. If being around men makes you feel worse, go into social hibernation for a day or two. If you feel especially domestic, save major housecleaning chores for that time of the month. If your nerves become too tense, ask your doctor for a mild tranquilizer. I've been told that sexual desire hits women the hardest around age thirty. Don't be afraid to discuss it with your doctor. To be forewarned is to be forearmed.

Hard work and exercise are excellent ways to help curb passion. Go swimming, play tennis, get out your bicycle or move the furniture around in the living room.

Spend time reading the Bible and praying. The psalms especially are full of verses that relate to the feeling level of our experience. "Lord, all my desire is before thee; and my groaning is not hid from thee," wrote the psalmist in Psalms 38:9 (KJV). Commit your feelings to God and be assured that He understands.

What kind of books and magazines do you read? A steady diet of "true confessions" and cheap sex novels will make things worse—not better.

Go shopping for a new dress. Keep busy with a hobby or other interest. Take a cold shower (don't knock it if you haven't tried it). Experiment with various activities and you will soon find what works best for you. None of these activities is a substitute for sex. They are simply constructive ways of controlling your sexual feelings until the time comes when they will be fulfilled in marriage.

By the way, self-control is not limited to single people. Married people must practice it, too. Suppose you are married and your husband comes home from work dead tired. You're ready to make whoopee. He's ready to collapse. Out of love and consideration for him—you practice self-control. Or perhaps your husband is sent overseas for several months, or you are suddenly widowed. Practice self-control now and you can practice it later on.

Avoid compromising situations. If being alone with a man in your apartment puts too much temptation in front of you, don't plan quiet evenings at home with him. I'll never forget the girl whose boyfriend was becoming too amorous and she decided they'd better have a talk. So she invited him over to her apartment. Before he arrived she lit a cozy fire in the fireplace, turned out all the lights in the living room and left only the hall light burning which cast a dim light into the room.

Who's kidding whom?

Be honest with yourself and your feelings. If you don't want trouble, then don't ask for it. A girl who goes braless, wears low-cut blouses and miniskirts, is asking for trouble—and down inside she knows it. All the words of protest in the world won't convince him that you're anything but a tease or a tramp.

Face the fact that *you* must set the standard for how far your lovemaking will go. In your dreams of the ideal man you may have pictured *him* as being the one to set and abide by the standards. But in real life that usually isn't the way things are. A man's passions are quickly aroused and powerfully strong, begging for gratification. He may *want* to do what's right, but when passion strikes he is sorely tempted to do otherwise. He *needs* the strength that you can provide by (a) not getting yourselves into compromising situations in the first place, (b) helping him keep the lid on his passions before things get out of hand, and (c) letting him know that *he can* control the situation, too. He shouldn't depend entirely upon you for control.

Let him know exactly what your standards are and stick to them. Don't let him talk you into doing anything you feel is wrong. He will test you with persuasive arguments to see how strong you really are. If you give in, he will lose respect for you and you will lose respect for yourself.

When you do fall in love, or even are just strongly attracted to a man, recognize in advance that holding the line is going to be difficult. It's easy to say, "Oh, I would never do *that*" when you haven't had a date in three years or your current date is a double drag. But when someone you really care about comes along, sleeping together will seem like the most natural thing in the world. Just because it seems natural, however, is no excuse for doing it before you get married. If you think otherwise, Satan is obviously at work.

Talk about every aspect of your relationship with the man you're going to marry. Pray together and separately that God will keep you both pure – and that He will be honored in every aspect of your relationship.

Masturbation

Most men and many women masturbate at some time in their lives. Once frowned upon as "dirty," it is now considered by many to be a normal part of the single life.

Interestingly enough, the Bible has nothing to say about masturbation as such. Every other form of normal and abnormal sex is mentioned including fornication, adultery, harlotry, homosexuality, beastiality, incest, and rape. But nowhere is anything said about masturbation.

This curious omission no doubt leads some people to believe that omission suggests permission. After all, they might reason, masturbation is hardly something invented in the twentieth century. If God doesn't condone it, why didn't He say so? In order to answer that, let's take a good hard look at the purpose of masturbation and some scriptural teachings that relate to it.

The purpose of masturbation is to provide relief for passion. We've already discussed the fact that there's nothing wrong with passion. But we've also discussed the fact that *normal sex* is the physical act that takes place between a man and woman. Any deviation from that norm is not a part of God's plan.

Masturbation is a marvelous way to train your body to become "a superb instrument of love," says the author of a well-known book on the art of being sensuous. Why is such training necessary? Because, she says, men are too impatient to train you themselves.

Where love is not involved in a sexual relationship, no doubt that last statement is true. A man gets what he came after and leaves when he's finished – with little or no thought for the woman he leaves behind. But when a man truly loves a woman he is as concerned about her feelings as about his own. When he gives himself to her he wants her to enjoy his body as much as he enjoys hers. One of the joys of married love is learning together the techniques of making love.

A woman who comes into marriage with a habit pattern of stimulation to orgasm already developed through masturbation robs herself of something beautiful. If there is one area of marriage where a man does *not* want to marry an expert, it is in the area of sex. If you are a virgin, you may feel hopelessly inadequate on your wedding night and wish you knew what to do next. But your husband is delighted with your inexperience. Together you will learn the joys of making love. The idea that women must train themselves in advance is sheer nonsense.

Sometimes masturbation becomes a substitute for normal dating relationships. A person who is normally shy about meeting people may retreat into a world of masturbation rather than making the effort to get out and meet people.

While the Bible is silent about the practice of masturbation, it does have something to say about the sexual fantasies that usually accompany masturbation.

Romantic and sexual thoughts are a normal part of every man and woman and have been since man was created. Who can deny the beauty of the Song of Solomon as the writer vividly expresses the love of a man for a woman? So explicit is the book that no Jew under thirty was allowed to read it.

When you love a man you naturally think about him in romantic terms. Besides that, there is a bit of the tigress in every woman and also a bit of the exhibitionist. Sexual fantasies, however, can quickly turn to lust. Prolonged thinking about sexual adventures with a man—whether he be real or imaginary—becomes a desire for someone who does not belong to you. And that is lust. Jesus said, "But I tell you that anyone who looks lustfully at a woman has in his heart already broken the marriage vow" (Matthew 5:28). The same applies to women.

Now let me hasten to say that a fleeting lustful thought is not sin. Satan continually tempts us with such thoughts. The secret is that the thought must be "fleeting." We are not responsible for the thoughts that enter our heads. But we are responsible for the ones that remain there. Martin Luther has suggested that you can't stop the birds from flying over your head, but you can prevent them from building a nest in your hair.

With or without masturbation, sexual fantasies can become a

habit pattern that is hard to break. Paul admonishes us, ". . . whatever is true, whatever is honorable, whatever is just, whatever is pure, whatever is lovely, whatever is kindly spoken, whatever is lofty and whatever is praiseworthy, put your mind on these" (Philippians 4:8). Are your sexual fantasies pretty intricate? The next time you are tempted in that direction, ask God to help you channel your imaginative ability into thoughts that are honoring to Him. The gift of imagination is the beginning of genius.

Another problem with both masturbation and sexual fantasies is the amount of time they take. As good stewards of God's gifts it is important that we use our time wisely. What good is it going to do you in the long run to stay home dreaming about a man when perhaps what you should be doing is going someplace where you'll meet one? Or what good will masturbation accomplish if what you should be doing instead is working out at the Y to get rid of those excess pounds?

Homosexuality

When Suzanne moved into an apartment with Joyce and Annette in a small Eastern city, Suzanne had no idea Joyce was a lesbian. It didn't take her long to find out. Suzanne was not a lesbian but had deep unmet needs for love and acceptance. She made no effort to date and had few friends besides her two roommates. Eventually the almost-inevitable happened. In a weak moment of sexual frustration and longing for love, Suzanne gave in to Joyce's demands and a homosexual relationship resulted. The relationship continued for many months until Suzanne could no longer stand the guilt. She broke off the relationship but before long the pattern repeated itself.

There is little evidence to support the theory that homosexuality is caused by either a hormone imbalance or heredity. There is overwhelming evidence indicating that homosexuality is the result of environment during the formative years of a child's life. Whatever the home life may have been, a lesbian has learned to fear men. She is driven away from heterosexual relationships into relationships with members of her own sex. She is attracted to other women. And she seeks out other women to fulfill her sexual needs. A true lesbian is caught in chains of desire so strong they control her life. Today's Gay Lib advocates aren't helping the matter. Recognition does not make it right.

Contrary to what most lesbians want you to believe, they can be cured. No lesbian is "stuck with her lot" unless she chooses to be. As proof that a cure is possible, let me tell you about Connie, one of the most dynamic Christian women I know — and an ex-lesbian.

For as long as Connie can remember she wanted to be a boy. As a child she dressed like a boy and tried to act like a boy. Her parents were alcoholics and her mother, she found out when she got older, was also a lesbian.

In her teen years Connie realized that her desires were not normal. She sought the help of several ministers, but none of them knew what to do for her. Finally she decided that if the ministers couldn't help her, maybe if she started dating boys her life would straighten out. So date she did — and she soon got pregnant. At sixteen she had a baby out of wedlock. Nearly three years later she gave her baby up for adoption. She couldn't bring herself to raise the child in the "hell" in which she was living.

In jail at nineteen, Connie met and "fell in love" with a woman who divorced her husband in order to live with Connie. For ten years the two women lived together while Connie posed as the father of the woman's two children. Her life revolved around alcohol, drugs, pretense (she even posed as a man at her job), and her lesbian activities. Miserable and hopeless, she tried twice to commit suicide. Both attempts were unsuccessful.

Finally one day when she was twenty-eight a series of events occurred which left Connie without money, friends, or drugs. Desperate and hopeless as the pains of withdrawal set in, she caught sight of an open church door. Racing for the door in a last desperate attempt for help, she was greeted by a Christian woman whose heart God had already prepared for Connie's arrival. Together they met with the assistant pastor who pointed Connie to the only One who could remake her twisted life. When she left the church that evening she was indeed a new creation. No more alcohol. No more drugs. And no more illicit sex.

Today Connie is one of the most radiant Christian women I know. Nearly every time I talk with her she has some exciting new thing to share that God is doing in her life. No longer is she attracted to women. Someday perhaps, in the providence of God, she will marry. She's certainly not opposed to the idea. The important thing, though, is that her twisted life has been made straight through the amazing power of God.

If you are caught in the chains of homosexuality, the same freedom that Connie has found can be yours if you will commit your life to Christ. A competent counselor can help you unhook the links in the chain. God Himself can make you a new person. The problem with many homosexuals, however, is that they don't really want to change. Paul tells us that "partakers in homosexuality . . . shall [not] inherit God's kingdom" (1 Corinthians 6:9, 10). That's a mighty big price to pay.

If you are living with a lesbian, by all means find another place to live. I am not suggesting that you disown your roommate just because she is involved in such a sin. Rather, you can help her and yourself best by not living with her. If her problem is that she is physically attracted to women, why should you put additional temptation in front of her? The sight of you in your slip or nightgown might be pretty hard on her. For your sake it's best that you live elsewhere, also. Given the right circumstances and setting, each of us is capable of any and every sin. Like Suzanne and Joyce, who's to say that you might not be tempted also— especially if your own background has placed you in desperate need of love.

Who's in Charge?

Like each of God's gifts, our physical desires were meant to serve us, not control us. And the only way you can control both your thoughts and your actions is by letting God control them for you. Put Him in charge of every aspect of your life—including your physical desires. Ask Him to channel your desires into activities that will bring honor to Him. He's ready and waiting to help.

*I'm single for a very special rea-
son. It is God's plan for me right
now. Perhaps I'm naive, but I think
that God provides the needed grace
for any position He puts us in. I look
forward to married life, but I also
enjoy single life.*

MILLIE (*age twenty-four*)

12

The Single I

*Celibacy Is for the Birds,
Or Is It?*

There are some single people in this world who would be better
off married. There are plenty of married people who would be
better off single.

Part of the problem lies in a misunderstanding of Paul's teaching about marriage and the single life. "Some statements in them
are hard to think through," said Peter. "The untaught and un-
steady twist those writings as they do the other Scriptures—to
their own ruin" (2 Peter 3:16).

The most misunderstood passage is 1 Corinthians 7. Let's
look at some of those verses.

It is well for a man to let the woman alone; but because of prevailing immorality let every man have his own wife and every
woman her own husband (1, 2). I say this by way of concession; not
as a regulation. I wish all men had my own attitude; but each person
has his own gift from God, the one in this direction, the other in
that. To the single and the widows I suggest that it is well for them
to remain as I am; but if they cannot restrain their passions, let

114

them marry, for it is better to marry than to be consumed by passion (6-9).

Regarding the virgins I have no divine injunction; but as one who has received mercy from the Lord to be trustworthy, I give my opinion. I consider, then, that in view of the impending distress it is well for a person to remain in his present situation. Are you united to a wife? Do not seek release. Are you unattached to a woman? Do not seek a wife. But in case you marry, you do not sin; nor does the virgin sin if she marries. Such, however, will experience physical trouble, and I would spare you that (25-28).

The single person is concerned with the Lord's affairs, how to please the Lord; but the married person is concerned with things of the world, how to please the wife; he has divided interests. As for the wife and the virgin, the unmarried woman is interested in the Lord's affairs, to be dedicated in body and spirit; but the married woman is concerned with things of the world, how she may please her husband. I mention this for your own interest, not to throw a noose over you, but to promote choice behavior and undisturbed devotion to the Lord (32-35).

A wife is bound to her husband (by the law) as long as he lives; but in case her husband dies, she is free to marry whom she pleases, — only in a Christian way. It is my judgment, however, that she will enjoy life better by remaining single. And I think that I, too, have God's Spirit (39, 40).

Some people would like you to believe that the single life is more acceptable to God than the married life. From these verses in 1 Corinthians they falsely deduce that if you *really* want to serve God, then you must remain single. To marry is, in essence, to admit your weakness. The truly holy life is the single one.

This view produces false guilt in some who really should marry. In order to remove the guilt feelings, they sublimate their desire for marriage until one day it comes crashing to the surface in most undesirable ways. Unfortunately, this view may also produce a self-righteous holier-than-thou attitude in the one holding the view.

On the other hand, some people who disregard 1 Corinthians 7 altogether, may be guilty of seeking marriage when they should remain single, or urging others to marry who possibly should not.

In order to understand Paul's teachings about marriage and celibacy, you must treat them as you do every other subject in Scripture—study them in context and along with all the other teachings in Scripture about marriage and celibacy. If you study any one passage alone, you can stack the evidence any way you want it to go. Take, for example, these passages regarding marriage.

Paul's Teachings	Other Scriptures
To the single and the widows I suggest that it is well for them to remain as I am. 1 Corinthians 7:8	The Lord God said: It is not good for the man to be alone; I will make him a suitable helper, completing him. Genesis 2:18
I wish all men had my own attitude. 1 Corinthians 7:7	He who has found a wife has gained a goodly portion, and obtains favor from the Lord. Proverbs 18:22
It is well for a man to let the woman alone. 1 Corinthians 7:1	Let marriage be held in honor by all and the marriage bed unpolluted. Hebrews 13:4

Having thus "proven" Paul to be antimarriage, let's try this next batch of verses on for size.

Paul's Teachings	Other Scriptures
I will therefore that the younger women marry, bear children, guide the house, give none occasion to the adversary to speak reproachfully. 1 Timothy 5:14 KJV	The disciples said to Him, "If such is the case of a man with his wife, it is preferable not to marry." Matthew 19:10

Paul's Teachings	Other Scriptures
On this account a man shall leave his father and mother and shall be joined to his wife, and the two shall become one flesh. Ephesians 5:31	It is better to live in the corner of a housetop than to share a house with a contentious woman. It is better to live in a desert land than with a contentious and fretful woman. Proverbs 21:9, 19
Nevertheless, let each and every one of you love his own wife as much as himself, so that the wife may revere her husband. Ephesians 5:33	I found more bitter than death the woman who is snares and nets at heart and whose hands are chains. Whoever pleases God will escape her; but the sinner will be ensnared by her. Ecclesiastes 7:26

I hope the point is obvious. The Bible as a whole talks about marriage as both good and bad — because there are both good and bad marriages. It encourages people to marry and it also encourages people to remain single. Because some people should marry and some should not.

It is hard to believe that God would not be in favor of marriage, since He is the One who instituted it in the first place. When He decided that it was not good for man to be alone, He could have created another man to keep Adam company. But He didn't. He made a woman. And the first marriage, with God's blessings, was the result.

When all of Paul's teachings about marriage are studied together, it becomes obvious that Paul is not antimarriage. In fact, he likens marriage to the relationship between Christ and the Church (*see* Ephesians 5). In no sense could that relationship be considered "second best."

Twice Paul qualifies his statements in 1 Corinthians 7: (1) "because of prevailing immorality [Corinth was a wicked seaport town] let every man have his own wife and every woman her own husband"; (2) "in view of the impending distress it is well for a person to remain in his present situation" [whether married or single]. Would he have made the same suggestions if the situation in Corinth had been different?

Paul says that the single person has more time for the Lord's work. The married person has divided interests. This is certainly true. For that very reason some missionaries (and others) have been called to be single so they can devote all of their time to preaching and teaching. Jesus said that some "have made themselves eunuchs for the kingdom of heaven's sake" (Matthew 19:12 KJV). But when 1 Corinthians 7 is studied along with Ephesians 5 and 6 you will see that Paul is not putting down marriage as offering no opportunity for Christian service. He compares the union between husband and wife to that of Christ and the Church and urges fathers to bring up their children in the nurture and admonition of the Lord (a solemn responsibility).

What shall we conclude then? The secret lies in 1 Corinthians 7:7: ". . . but each person has his own gift from God, the one in this direction, the other in that." For some God's gift is marriage. For others it is to remain single. And the only gift mentioned in Scripture that is said to be better than all others is the gift of love. To marry or not to marry is an individual matter between you and God. No one else can decide it for you. And you cannot decide it for someone else.

To Marry or Not to Marry

So how do you decide whether or not you are to marry? The same way you discover any other gift God may choose to give you (see 1 Corinthians 12). First you commit your will completely to Him. And then you wait to see what gift He will send your way.

Ah, but that commitment. That's the rub, isn't it? Because marriage is a very emotional matter and there are very few of us who do not crave it. How, then, can we really commit something that is so dear to our hearts?

Commitment is possible only if you *trust* God. Do you really trust Him? Enough to say, "God, if You want me to marry, then show me the man of Your choice" (that's the easy part) and "God, if You want me to be single, I'll be single for Your glory" (that's the hard part). Do you love Him and trust Him enough to leave the gift-giving up to Him? If He does want you to be single, does that mean you're going to be miserable for the rest of your life? Of course not. If the gifts God gives only brought misery, He wouldn't be God. If He wants you to be single, you'll be content. Can you trust Him for that? If you do honestly commit the matter to Him and the strong desire for marriage persists, chances are that's an indication God wants you to marry and will permit you to marry when the time is right.

Commitment of the matter has to be complete and unqualified or it isn't really commitment. Bargaining with God won't work. I remember one of my college professors telling how it wasn't until his wife finally surrendered to God her desires to marry that her future husband came along. And I immediately thought, "Aha, if I commit it to God, along will come my man." And then I realized that that was bargaining with God. "I'll do such and such, Lord, if You'll do this." That's not trusting. That's bargaining. And God can see right through it.

There is a risk involved in trust because you and I can't see the future. We only know that right *now* we want to get married. But trust begets trust. Think back over your life since you found Christ. Has God ever let you down? *Ever?* Make a list of all the times you went out on a limb and really trusted God. Did He saw the limb out from under you? Of course not. Chances are He worked things out so much better than you anticipated you could hardly believe it. All right, then, if He didn't let you down in the past, is He likely to let you down in the future? Is God a cruel God, denying you the really good things in life and offering you only the bad? Your concept of God determines just how much you are able to trust Him.

Commitment doesn't mean saying to yourself: "Well, looks like I'm going to be single for the rest of my life. Whoopee. I can hardly wait to go through life alone, alone, alone." Who *says* you're going to be single forever? The point is, are you willing to be single *for as long as God wants you to be single?*

What happens if you refuse to trust God in the matter? Chances are you will do one of three things:

You might decide (consciously or unconsciously) to sublimate your feelings and refuse to face up to your true desires. Pushing aside your desire to marry before you've faced up to it is dangerous because one of these days it will raise its head like an ugly monster. How many girls have panicked when they reached their thirties or forties and married the first guy who came along? All those years they may have been trying to convince themselves they were happy single. Then along comes a guy with super charm, arousing emotions that have lain dormant for years, and they're off and running—to the altar. Wise judgments are rarely made in a state of panic.

Or you might decide if God isn't going to provide you with a husband, then you'll take matters into your own hands. Maybe you decide that having an affair is the answer. Or you start giving far too much attention to a dog or cat. An animal can become a substitute for the love and affection you desire from a man. (Now don't rush out and take your cat to the pound. Just treat animals like animals, not human beings.)

Or you may simply decide to wallow in self-pity and feed your soul on bitterness and resentment. Not a very pretty thought. Not a very pretty you.

God isn't going to force you to commit anything to Him. The choice is strictly up to you. That's the freedom He gives you because He wants you to trust Him.

When you do surrender your will to Him, a whole new world will open up. You won't need to fear the future anymore or waste valuable energy worrying about whether or not you will marry. God has promised that He will "guide thee continually, and satisfy thy soul . . ." (Isaiah 58:11 KJV). Nobody can satisfy a soul quite like God, not even a husband. But a husband can help, if that is God's choice for you.

The Most Important Single Man in Your Life

Did you ever stop to think about the fact that Jesus Christ was single? Since He was human as well as divine, He experienced the same things you and I have experienced in the single life. No doubt at times He longed for a wife and children. But I'm sure He never let His mind dwell on such thoughts because He knew it wouldn't serve any useful purpose. He didn't moan about His condition. He simply accepted the fact that God could use Him best unmarried.

Why do you think God chose to let Christ remain single? He could just as easily have provided Him with a wife and children. His mother Mary was strong enough to bear the pain of losing her Son on the cross. Wasn't there another woman strong enough to bear the loss of a husband?

The answer, of course, is obvious. Jesus Christ had a goal in life, a job to do, which was best done without the added responsibilities of marriage. His life on earth was a brief one. He had a job to do that had eternal ramifications. He put all of His energies into it. And because He did, you and I and anyone else who accepts Him as Lord and Saviour will never be the same.

What is the job God has given *you* to do? Is it possible that God can best use you single at this particular time in your life? Are you willing to place your life in the hands of the greatest single Man who ever lived?

But I Really Need a Man

Of course you do. You need to be around men. You need to communicate with a man. Can God take care of those needs, too?

Audrey Lee Sands, in her book *Single & Satisfied*, tells how God met those very needs for her on the mission field when she committed her single life to Him.

By the end of my first year on the field, though still very happy in the work, I began to feel deep depression resulting from lack of companionship and friendship with the opposite sex. It was a feeling of inadequacy, a feeling that no man would ever really want me anyhow. But our Lord has a great understanding heart. Right at that time a fine young man paid a prolonged visit to a neighboring missionary family. Our paths quickly crossed. We were of kindred minds and enjoyed each other's fellowship to the full. He was a pleasure to be with, and he knew how to treat a woman like a queen without leading her on.

That short period of masculine companionship fully restored my lost confidence in my own femininity. The depression lifted. When he left, I missed him, and commitments had to be strengthened with the Lord; but I saw the wonderful hand of the Heavenly Father in allowing me that time. He had not been trying to downgrade me as a woman. He only wanted me to trust him more fully to meet those womanly needs.

God wants you to be a complete person. And He knows that male companionship (whether temporary or permanent) is necessary for a balanced life. He can and will meet those needs, too.

Trust Him.

The best place to meet the right man is in the center of God's will.

AUTHOR UNKNOWN

13

Where Have All the Young Men Gone?

Where and How to Meet Men

Every now and again I read some morbid statistic which says there are X number more women than men in the United States. The conclusion produced by the statistic is that there just aren't enough men to go around—unless you head for some remote outpost where the men miraculously outnumber the women.

With all due respect for statistics I seriously doubt that any single Christian woman in America will remain single solely because there aren't enough men to go around. God has a plan for your life. And if that plan includes marriage, then He will provide the right man.

But where to find those eligible men is something else. In the big cities they are all around. But if you are living in some podunk town off in nowhere, chances are you haven't seen an interesting male in quite a spell. Relax. There's hope!

But before we talk about *where* to find men, I think we'd better talk about just who it is you're looking for. As a Christian, the field is somewhat narrower for you than for your non-Christian girl friends. A Christian can't marry just anybody.

There were two admonitions regarding dating when I was growing up: Never date a non-Christian. Never date anyone who could not be a potential mate. If you grew up in a conservative home or church, chances are you heard the same admonitions.

And they aren't bad advice for teen-agers who do not always have the maturity necessary to keep their emotions in check. Following those admonitions could save some young person from a lot of grief.

But what about you? You aren't a teen-ager anymore. However, choosing the right marriage partner is just as important as it was when you were pre-twenty. Do those two admonitions still apply?

First of all, let me say this. Dating non-Christians *is* risky business. I'm not saying you shouldn't date them. But realize when you do that if non-Christian Mr. Dream Stuff is everything you've ever wanted in a man in every *other* way, his spiritual condition may suddenly become less important. If you marry him, no matter how wonderful he is, you will still be married to an unbeliever. And Paul is quite correct when he asks how a believer can have fellowship with an unbeliever. Once the glamour has worn off, spiritually speaking you will each be going your separate ways. (No, don't think you can convert him once you get married. In fact if you do try to convert him you will probably only drive him further away.) The most important factor in marriage is having Jesus Christ as your Head. Without Him you have an extremely shaky foundation for marriage and child-rearing.

While I urge extreme caution in dating non-Christians, I must acknowledge that sometimes God may allow you to date such a person for a very special reason. Perhaps it is to teach you something, perhaps to teach the other person. But God can use you in such a situation only if you are mature in your relationship with Him.

A most touching illustration of this is the story of Ginger. While doing graduate work, she met a paraplegic man—non-Christian, divorced, but attractive. They hit it off immediately and began to date. And before long they fell in love. Ginger shared her faith in Christ with John, but as a Christian she knew the problems involved if they were to marry. She also knew that she loved him.

When her schooling was finished, Ginger left for home some

three thousand miles away. She and John corresponded until the time came when he could come and see her. The big reunion was just days away—but he never arrived. He, too, knew the problems involved, and called to tell her it was better that he not come. Some months later he had surgery—and died on the operating table.

Heartbroken, but still trusting God, Ginger traveled the three thousand miles back to the hospital where John had died. She visited the head nurse whom she knew and discovered to her joy that shortly before his death John had accepted Christ. No doubt this was the result of her sharing Christ with him many months before.

The pain Ginger suffered was real. But because of her maturity and dependence upon God, He was able to use her for a special mission.

The other admonition I learned was never to date anyone who could not be a potential mate. The only trouble with that suggestion is that often it's pretty hard to tell just who is mate material and who isn't. If a guy is a homosexual, an alcoholic, or a drug addict, it's pretty obvious he's a bad date/mate risk. But for the most part you can't really know what a man is like until you've dated him several times. That quiet guy who looks like Dullsville Unlimited may turn out to be an interesting conversationalist when he's away from the crowd. Except for the obvious derelicts, don't write anybody off until you've given him a chance. You wouldn't want some nice man to write *you* off after one date, would you?

The important thing is that whoever you marry be mature and a Christian. And obviously whoever you marry will be someone you first date. Give each guy a chance for the first date or two, then be selective about future dates.

Where to Meet Men

Now for the part you've all been waiting for. Where *are* those smashingly wonderful men? First of all I'll tell you one place they aren't. They aren't on your doorstep.

"You've got to get out where they are," my mother kept telling me when I was single. "They aren't going to come knocking on your door." And she was absolutely right. It was much easier to stay home and watch TV or have dinner with a girl friend than to try and drum up dates. But had I stuck to that secure little routine I wouldn't be married to a super wonderful man today. You have to get out where they are.

And eligible men are just about everywhere. You may not see them at first glance but they're there. Among my many married friends, one met her man in a bowling alley. One met hers through a blind date arranged by her boss. One met hers in a small church they both attended. My husband and I and many of our friends met in a church single adult group. As long as you are in the center of God's will, Mr. Right could turn up most anywhere. There are a few specific places, however, where you might have a better chance of meeting some interesting men.

Special-interest clubs Is skiing your thing? Why not join a ski club? You may not marry the ski instructor but you might at least meet someone who will pick up the pieces if you smash a ski. Or maybe you've got the travel bug. Or you really dig drama. There are special-interest clubs for tall people, short people, and everybody in between. Check the Yellow Pages or ask a friend with a similar interest and see what's available in your locale. But don't join unless you're really interested in the subject. A man-hungry hanger-on will not be appreciated in a club full of people who really dig bird watching.

Study courses If you're not ready for the special-interest club, maybe you need to cultivate a hobby. How about a beginning course in photography, cooking (check first to make sure it's not a girls-only class), gardening, medieval art, or Elizabethan poetry? A friend tells me she and her husband are taking a woodworking class, and the class is loaded with bachelors and single women. Call or write local colleges and universities and see what's available. Even if you don't meet anyone interesting on the first try, new knowledge about a subject will make you a more interesting conversationalist. And a new hobby or skill never hurt anybody.

Sports When was the last time you played tennis, went bowling, swam at a public pool, or went bicycling? If you aren't the athletic type, you'll have to work at it. Besides being good exercise which will help you stay healthy and trim, you never know who may turn up on the other side of the tennis court or swimming pool. And this is a good place to reemphasize one thing: Don't always go everywhere in the company of a girl friend or a flock of girls. Once in awhile do something all by yourself. You can bowl alone, bicycle alone, swim alone, and hit your tennis ball against the backboard 187 times all by yourself. Most guys are at least a little bit shy. If the only way to meet you is to fight his way through the mob, most guys won't make the effort.

Vacations Where did you go on your vacation last year? Home to spend two dull weeks with good old mother and dad? By all means visit your parents *sometime,* but unless the old hometown is loaded with men you aren't going to have a very exciting vacation. Now is the time to see the world. Save your pennies carefully and with today's low air fares, there's hardly anywhere you can't afford to go. Europe. The Holy Land. The Orient. Or an African safari. And don't forget the U.S.A.

If you're brave enough to hoof it on your own, more power to you. If not, join a travel club. Make sure it's a reputable one and check first to see what type of people usually join the club's tours. Three weeks with a group of senior citizens or little old ladies from Iowa isn't going to be too productive.

Zsa Zsa Gabor (well, she *has* met quite a few men in her time) says the last place to look for a man is on a cruise ship. Stick to air travel. About the only thing you find on a cruise, she says, is other women looking for the romantic adventure advertised in the travel brochure and a bunch of crew members who are blasé from so much attention by the women. Outside of Aristotle Onassis, most busy men don't have time to take a cruise. And remember, if you sign up for a three-week cruise, you're stuck with whoever turns up on board (or doesn't turn up) for *three full weeks.*

If possible, join a tour that allows you to meet the people in all or most of the countries you visit. My first trip to Europe was a three-week bus tour of so many countries I've nearly lost count. We spent much of our time shuttling on and off the bus, counting noses, and hurtling through those narrow European streets trying to get from one place to another. The only "natives" I met were the bus driver and the tour guide—both married.

My next trip to Europe and the Middle East was with my husband. What a contrast from that first trip! We spent the first three weeks with a small tour group during which time we had dinner in the home of an Egyptian family in Cairo, visited in the home of a family in Nazareth, and ate dinner prepared by Christian Arabs on the top of a watchtower in a vineyard near Jerusalem. During the next three and a half weeks when we traveled on our own we met a British couple on the way to London and visited in the homes of previously unknown relatives in the north of Scotland. You never really see a country until you meet the people who live there.

Many tourist offices sponsor meet-the-people programs in different countries. Perhaps you've seen them listed in travel brochures—"Don't Miss the Swiss," "Know the Norwegians," "Find the Finns," "Get in Touch with the Dutch." Write to the nearest branch of the travel office of the country you plan to visit and ask if they have such a program. Give them your name, age, profession, the date you plan to arrive, how long you will be in a particular city or country and your interests. The tourist office maintains a list of volunteer hosts and will attempt to match you up with people of similar interests. Entertainment is up to the host, but you'll undoubtedly at least be invited to dinner in his or her home. Take a small thank-you gift and don't expect free bed and board.

In her book, *The Intelligent Woman Traveler,* Frances Koltun lists a variety of special-interest groups for everybody from teachers to veterinarians who will take you under their wing. Check the appendix of her book for names and addresses in the country you plan to visit.

Computer dating clubs   The advent of the computer dating club is a happy circumstance. Some people may look askance at such a view, but I see nothing unspiritual about letting a machine find somebody interesting for you to date. In no way does the machine replace the leading of the Lord in finding you a mate. Once you've met No. 1473698 it's still up to you to decide whether or not he's Mr. Right.

There are two distinct advantages to computer dating clubs, to my way of thinking. One advantage is for single people who live in small towns where there is little or no opportunity to meet other singles. There you are dutifully teaching school in a microscopic town of 750 people. Not a single man in sight. Eighty miles away there's a single man working in a similar small town, every bit as lonely for companionship as you are. Without the help of a computer dating club you two might never meet. Read the letters written to the clubs and you'll discover that such matches really do happen.

The second advantage is this: it's an awfully easy way to get a date and requires a minimum of effort on your part. No running around from singles group to singles group (though by no means should you shut off contact with the outside world once you join a computer club). No matter what you look like or how bad your hair looks at the moment, once the computer pulls your card you've as good as got a date. Of course, the next step is definitely up to you. No laziness permitted. How you look and act on that first date determines whether or not Mr. C. will ever call you again. If you're in a slow period with few interesting men looking your way, a computer dating club could be a big boost to your morale.

Because dating non-Christians is such risky business, I would not recommend the usual assortment of computer clubs. However, I can recommend The Compliment Club (Hopkins Building, Mellott, Indiana 47958). This nationwide computer dating club tries to match people of the same denomination and promises that it "will *not* knowingly attempt to match people of radically different races, color, or religion."

To join you will complete an application form and supply three character references. You will be interviewed by a field counselor (usually a minister in your area) and pay a one-time fee of $25. The club tries to match people who live within one- or two-hundred miles of each other to minimize travel expense.

Christian single adult groups   I was twenty-eight and still single and I decided those two factors must be a good indication there was something wrong with me. So I made an appointment to see a counselor. At the first session I poured out my tale of woe. To compound the age and singleness factors, I was working in a small church where the only men available were college age (too young) and a bachelor nearly twenty years my senior (too old). I hadn't had an honest-to-goodness date with a man my age in longer than I cared to remember.

My counselor understood my plight because he himself had married later in life. So he suggested I start attending the single adult group at a local church where he and his wife had met. I took his advice and a whole new world opened up. I didn't know there were that many single men left in the world! And within about two weeks I had a date. Not because there was anything drastically delightful about my personality. But because at last I was available — not tucked away where no eligible men existed. I spent three or four years in that singles group, then gradually migrated to the single adult group at another church where I met my husband. Today we belong to a group composed of couples, most of whom met each other in that single adult group.

If you are dutifully working in or attending a small church which has no single adult group, your chances of meeting eligible Christian men, as you well know, are extremely limited. If there are several singles in your church, why not band together and form a single adult group? You might consider contacting other small churches in your area and set up a group that reaches singles in all of these churches. If this is not possible, investigate the groups offered by larger churches in your area. You *need* the fellowship of people your own age — both male and female. When you join such a group, however, it must be with a greater purpose than just to find a man. A strong evangelical group can have an important ministry to both Christian and non-Christian singles who are attracted to it. Get involved!

Christian conferences for singles   In addition to church single-adult groups, some Christian camp and conference centers schedule retreats and conferences for single adults. This is a good opportunity to meet singles from many churches. Listed below are conference centers that plan their own conferences for singles. Still others make their facilities available for churches and denominations which plan conferences for singles. Find out what is available in your area and take advantage of these opportunities to learn more about God, His Word, and His children.

Mount Hermon Christian Conference Center
Mount Hermon, California 95041

Campus Crusade for Christ
Arrowhead Springs
San Bernardino, California 92414
(Single's Lay Institute for Evangelism)

Hume Lake Christian Camps
P.O. Box 2267
Fresno, California 93720

Hawaii Christian Camp and Conference Association
Box 6055
Honolulu, Hawaii 96818

Gull Lake Bible and Missionary Conference
Box 1
Hickory Corners, Michigan 49060

Monadnock Bible Conference
Dublin Rd.
Jaffrey Center, New Hampshire 03454

Word of Life
Island Camp
Schroon Lake, New York 12870

Pine Cove
Rt. 8
Tyler, Texas 75701

The Firs
4605 Cable St.
Bellingham, Washington 98225

You may also write to the Sunday School Department, Sunday School Board of the Southern Baptist Convention, 127 Ninth Avenue, North, Nashville, Tennessee 37234 for information about the annual single adult conferences they conduct at two locations:

Glorieta Baptist Conference Center
Glorieta, New Mexico 87535

Ridgecrest Baptist Conference Center
Ridgecrest, North Carolina 28770

Married friends   I'm purposely listing married friends at the bottom of the list of ways to meet men. Sometimes married friends are helpful. Too often, however, they don't do you any favors. "I've got this friend I'd like to fix you up with," they say. And your eyes light up. Before long up rolls Blind Date No. 24 and he's just what you expected—a disaster.

Personally, I never had much luck with blind dates, though some of my friends have. Either the guy wasn't interested in me or I couldn't stand him. My most notable disaster was arranged by someone I never met. (Probably just as well!) A meeting was agreed upon by both parties and a letter arrived asking if he could come see me just before Christmas (he lived two states away). Before I had time to answer he called me long distance to arrange the time. How romantic, I thought. This is just like a storybook romance. Somehow I managed to survive until Christmas and the day he was to arrive. Through five hundred miles of snow he drove—just to meet *me!* When he arrived my romantic hopes were instantly dashed. I hadn't expected a man who wore rubbers over his cowboy boots. The meeting progressed steadily downhill from then on.

Ann Landers (or is it Abigail Van Buren?) has an excellent piece of advice you might like to pass on to your married friends who are eager to fix you up with someone: Never arrange a date for your single friends unless you are doing both parties a favor.

How to Meet Men

And now for a few practical tips on how to meet men. You're surrounded by eligibles. Your big moment has arrived. And—you're tongue-tied. How do you start a conversation with a man when your voice box has gone numb and your knees are noticeably knocking?

Look your best The first step is to make sure you look and feel good. I read or heard some advice once that really stuck with me: Always dress and groom yourself as if *today* were the day you were going to meet Mr. Right. (You might, you know.) Think about that when you get dressed in the morning. It may mean changing your panty hose, even if the run is on the inside, washing your hair a little oftener, checking for split seams or kicked-out hems, and ironing the rump-sprung out of your skirts. If you look good, you'll feel good. If you look a mess, your self-confidence will be batting zero.

Think about him I don't mean stand there and think wildly romantic thoughts about that man you're dying to meet. A rapidly beating heart might be detected even through your clothing. Could be a little embarrassing. What I do mean is to remember that *he* is probably just as nervous about meeting new people as you are. If taking the initiative in starting a conversation will help put him at ease, do it. If both of you stand there shuffling your feet you won't accomplish much.

Look for ways to break the ice A close girl friend spotted my husband before I ever met him and decided that he and I were made for each other. (She was dating one of my husband's best friends whom she later married.) For months she kept telling me that I really should start attending the single adult group they both belonged to and meet George because he was such a great guy. Finally I decided I'd better take her advice. So I went to one of their meetings.

There we were in a roomful of people. Now how do we get together? I had a plan.

George is an artist. I am a writer. I had just been asked by the director of Christian education at our church to put together a monthly newsletter for the Sunday-school staff. I could do the writing. But the paper also needed a name and some artwork for the logo. Who could possibly be better to do the artwork than that charming artist who works for Walt Disney? And what better way to get acquainted than with a legitimate request for his help?

When the moment was right I followed him across the room as he moved from a conversation with someone to the refreshment table. "I'm chasing you," I said softly into his ear and when he turned around (slightly in shock) I proceeded to tell him about the newsletter. We sat down and discussed what was needed (and a few other things!) as he sketched some ideas for the logo and helped me come up with a title. One thing led to another as the days went by. He came over to my office to bring the artwork and we talked some more. He asked me for a date. And ten and one half months later we were married.

Suppose you're at an ice rink and there's an interesting man there that you'd like to meet. If he doesn't take the initiative in getting acquainted, maybe you'll have to. First be sure he isn't with a date—or a wife! When you're sure the coast is clear, skate up to him the next time he stops to tighten a skate and say, "You skate very well. Are you a skating instructor?" If that doesn't appeal to his male ego, nothing will! Suppose after a few laps around the rink he asks to take you home. If you say yes you've become a pickup and a mature woman never needs to resort to that. If *he* can pick you up he'll figure *any* man could. He'll respect you more if you follow normal dating procedures. If he no longer interests you, say no, thank you. If you'd like to see him again, say, "I'm afraid I can't, but I come here every Thursday (if you do). Perhaps I'll see you again." If he's really interested he'll be back next Thursday and you'll have a chance to get better acquainted before accepting a date.

Be feminine   Whatever approach you take must be decidedly you and fit your personality. If you don't feel right about taking the initiative or are not the type who can carry it off, then don't do it. Femininity is a precious commodity which can easily be destroyed if you become too aggressive. Once the ice is broken, let him do the pursuing from then on. If you find yourself continually taking the initiative in conversation and activities with a particular man under the faint hope that he might be, or become, interested in you, it's time to face reality. If he were really interested in you, *he* would take the initiative.

Let him catch your eye   That delicious-looking man is sitting across the room from you and you're dying to meet him. Every time he looks at you, you look away. And every time you look at him, *he* looks away. That's not the way progress is made. The next time you feel him looking at you, look directly at him for just a moment and smile, then look away. Once he's made eye contact he will feel more at ease about starting a conversation.

In the single adult group where George and I met there was a very attractive girl. I wondered out loud one time why he had never dated her. The answer was simple. "I could never even catch her eye," he said. "And a guy's got to be able to at least catch a girl's eye before he feels like trying to get acquainted with her."

Listen, listen, listen   Once you do start talking to a man, keep him talking—about himself. Ask questions to draw him out. Go beyond the obvious questions of "Where do you work?" "What do you do?" to questions that probe, ever so gently, how he *feels* about what he does. The male ego is a delicate object. You can strengthen his self-confidence immeasurably by showing genuine interest in the things he tells you. To do this successfully, however, you must be genuinely interested in people in general, as well as him in particular.

In her book, *How to Talk with Practically Anybody About Practically Anything,* Barbara Walters tells of the time she found herself seated next to Aristotle Onassis at a luncheon. She sat there absolutely tongue-tied, unable to think of any suitable questions to ask this world-famous man. Finally she decided to give it a try. Grabbing a break in the heavy nautical talk going on about her she said, "Tell me, Mr. Onassis, you're so success-ful — not just in shipping and airlines, but in other industries, too — I wonder, how did you begin? What was your very first job?"

Mr. Onassis was delighted with the question and launched into animated discussion of his early emigration to Argentina and his jobs there as a dishwasher, construction worker, and cigarette salesman, which eventually led to his first fortune. (Pick up a copy of that book for some very practical tips on how to talk to people.)

Be yourself   Don't belittle yourself. Don't pretend to be some-thing you aren't. Just be you. Because I had more education than many of the men I dated, I often felt like I had to play myself down. Which accomplished nothing except to frustrate me. When my husband came along he accepted me just the way I am. I'd have been a whole lot better off if I had done the same long before I met him. If you try to be something you aren't, you may miss out when Mr. Right comes looking for the real you.

You probably bought the book for this chapter. But please don't stop reading. The next chapter is the most important chapter in the book.

I have come so they may have life
and have it abundantly.

John 10:10

14

The Balanced Life

Getting It All Together —
and Keeping It There

It's a beautiful day, the sun is shining, and you haven't a care in the world. Good day for a drive, you decide, and off you go in your trusty car. All's well until the speedometer reaches sixty or sixty-five and your car comes down with a classic case of the shakes. It feels like your tires have suddenly gone square. If you continue to drive with it that way, the rubber on the tires will wear unevenly and you may end up with a flat. There's only one way to remedy the situation. Take the car to a garage and have the tires balanced and the front end aligned.

The abundant life that Jesus promised is a balanced life because your will is aligned with His. Anybody can have a balanced natural life — eating the right food, getting proper rest and recreation, etc. But alignment is spiritual — your will aligned with God's. One without the other produces the same result — worn-out tires and a bumpy ride through life.

The abundant life is full of ups and downs, curves and straight stretches, rough roads and smooth ones. Like the Ziggy cartoon I read the other day, at times you may feel, "Every time I get it all together — somebody moves it." But the difficult times in life are easier to bear when your life is aligned with Christ's.

The balanced life begins with:

137

Forgiveness

Perhaps someone reading this book has never met Jesus face-to-face. You've been going your own way, doing your own thing, with little regard for the One who loves you more than any human being will ever love you. He loved you so much, in fact, that He chose death—and Resurrection—that you might live. And He promised that the life He wants to give you will be abundant, balanced, a life you could never find on your own. "I am the Way and the Truth and the Life;" Jesus said, "no one comes to the Father except through Me" (John 14:6). Your new life begins when you commit all that you are and have and hope to be to Jesus Christ. Ask Him to take away the sin that is within you and replace it with the cleansing power of His Holy Spirit.

When Jesus Christ enters your life, He forgives you of every sin you have ever committed. That's a pretty big order when you stop to think about it. But can you imagine God ever carrying a grudge? When we repent of the wrong that we have done, He unconditionally forgives us. Never does He say, "I forgive" one day and then bring up the issue again tomorrow. He forgives. And He forgets.

But we can't. Forget, that is. And sometimes we don't forgive ourselves either. Are you still blaming yourself for some sin in the past? Do you continually mull over past mistakes? "Satan, as usual, is the author of extremes," says Dr. Dwight Carlson in his book *Run and Not Be Weary*. "He would either like us to be happy-go-lucky, indifferent Christians or else carrying an awful, dreaded, heavy burden, making the Christian life a real drag."

If you are unable to forgive yourself for some past sin, then I doubt if you have ever really accepted God's forgiveness. Because if you had, you would have no reason to not forgive yourself. Are you more important than God? If He can forgive you, why can't you forgive yourself?

The psalmist said, "Create in me a clean heart, O God, and renew a steadfast spirit within me" (Psalms 51:10). Once forgiven, He acts upon that forgiveness and promises to "teach

transgressors Thy ways, and sinners shall be converted to Thee"
(Psalms 51:13). He shares his forgiveness with others. His life is
living proof that God has forgiven him and he has forgiven himself. ". . . men should repent and turn to God and live lives to
prove their change of heart" (Acts 26:20 PHILLIPS).

The balanced life also involves forgiving others. That's a tough
one. It's easy to forgive the "nice" person who accidentally steps
on your toes. But how about the "not so nice" person who continually steps on your toes and makes no attempt to apologize?
Do you really have to forgive that person, too?

Yes. Because being a Christian means forgiving others, no
matter what they do to you. Did your father desert the family
when you were small and you've never forgiven him? Is your
mother a domineering old lady who drives you up the wall? Did
your best friend steal your boyfriend (or at least you think she
did) and you'll resent her sneaky tricks as long as you live?

Refusal to forgive a person for something he has done wrong
actually means that you are harboring resentment toward him.
And resentment is a terribly destructive force. What the person
did to you is not nearly as important as the resentment you are
hoarding. For you see, the person who wronged you can live
quite happily without your forgiveness (provided he has asked
God for forgiveness). But *you* will *never* be happy as long as you
harbor resentment. To forgive a person puts you on top of things.
To refuse to forgive puts you at the very bottom of the heap.

Okay, suppose your mother *is* a domineering old lady. It's
often difficult to separate obnoxious mannerisms from the person.
If your mother tries to tell you every move to make, of course you
aren't going to like that. Nobody expects you to. But can you
accept her as she is anyway, look a little harder for her good
points, forgive her for the wrong she does — and go on from there?
Your failure to accept her and forgive her may be part of the reason she acts the way she does. People who feel unloved do some
mighty strange things sometimes. Did you ever stop to think
about that?

I'm not saying forgiveness is always easy. But I do know that
when you finally become willing to commit the matter to God,

He will make it possible for you to forgive. If He can forgive you, it's for sure He can forgive others through you.

The balanced life also includes:

Purpose

The chief end of man, says the Shorter Catechism, is "to glorify God and to enjoy him for ever." You didn't just happen. You are here for a reason — to glorify God and enjoy Him. Isn't it nice that there are two parts to that purpose? The more you enjoy Him the more you want to glorify Him.

What does it mean to "glorify" God? That word used to bother me because it seemed like such a general term and I wanted to know the specifics. But that's just the point. To glorify God means that in everything you do and say, you step out of the way so that others can see Christ. If you really want to glorify God it will affect the way you dress, the things you do, what you say, where you go. Glorifying God touches every aspect of life.

Glorifying God does not mean that you have to buttonhole every person you meet and pump them full of the gospel. Some people have the mistaken idea that God has called them to convert the world single-handedly. And if they don't witness verbally to everyone they meet, they feel guilty.

For two years before I got married the same beautician did my hair nearly every week. Week after week I sat there trying to figure out some way to witness to her. And week after week the opportunity just wasn't there. Often I would leave the shop wondering if there was something wrong with me. Was I a coward at heart? Or wasn't the time right to witness to her?

Finally after two years the opportunity fell into my lap. My beautician and a couple of others were discussing religion and one of them asked me what I believed. Out poured the plan of salvation and they all listened because *they* had asked, not because I had forced the issue. But it took two years before that happened.

A similar experience with a neighbor convinced me of the uselessness of worrying about witnessing. If your heart is tuned to God and you are concerned about others, He will provide the opportunities for you to share your faith. If you try to force the issue, you will only do damage. Letting the Holy Spirit control your witnessing efforts takes the strain off of you and will make things more natural when it is time to say a word. In the meantime, of course, your life must back up what you say.

And that brings us to the matter of:

Goals

It's pretty difficult to work out God's purpose for a balanced life without some goals — both long-range and short-range. How can you best glorify God? By furthering your education? Learning a new skill? Taking up a new hobby? Spending a few pennies on a charm-school course to make you a more pleasant person to be around? Taking a Bible study course at a Christian school? Joining a political or civic group where you will meet non-Christians? (It's so easy to bask in the shelter of our nice little church groups.)

What do you expect to accomplish in the next three months? The next year? The next five years? Ask God to show you what kind of goals you should set. Then work on them until you have achieved what you set out to do. If, in the process, God should direct you into a new goal, that's all right, too. The important thing is to aim at something constructive. Otherwise, you'll never get anywhere. There is a tremendous sense of accomplishment when you achieve a goal in life.

The balanced life is also:

Others-Centered

The happiest people in the world are those who put other people first (second only to Christ). When was the last time you did something to help someone? Remember how good it made you feel? Getting involved with other people is one of the most rewarding experiences of life.

If you think nobody could possibly need you, take a look around. Everywhere there are people who need help. Hospitals need volunteer workers. Churches need Sunday-school teachers, choir members, and a host of other workers. How about getting a group together and planning a party for children in an orphanage? Or taking some of the children on outings to the zoo, the beach, or some other place of interest? There's no excuse for staying inside your shell when the whole wide world is crying for your help.

Spend time with families as well as with your single friends. If the husband and wife get along well, their home can provide a valuable stabilizing effect in your life. And you in turn can be of help to them. How about taking the kids to the park some Saturday so the parents can have a little time to themselves? (A word of caution: if the husband and wife don't get along, keep your distance.)

The woman who only thinks of herself is hardly pleasant company, because her life is off-balance. I'll never forget the single woman who lived next door to me one time. She was well on her way to becoming a hypochondriac. "Look," she said to me one day, pulling up her skirt to show me the back of her thigh. "My flesh is quivering." (Heaven help her!) She was a Christian— but a bit self-centered!

There are times, however, when it is in the best interests of yourself and others to call, "Time out!" and spend a little time with yourself. Some people get so others-centered that their lives get off-balance in that direction, too. They operate under the misconception that to be others-centered means you must be continually on the go. They run from one activity to another, always rushed for time, always a little out of breath. They fail to realize that if you are really going to help others you need to look after yourself as well. That means proper rest, quiet meals (instead of always on the run), time spent along with the Lord and His Word, and time spent alone with yourself.

Frantic activity (even when it's for legitimate reasons) may actually be a means of escape from the problems of life. Dedication to a Christian organization does not guarantee dedication to Christ. Service to others does not guarantee spiritual growth. If it is simply an escape hatch, it can actually detract from spiritual growth. There are times when you need to pamper yourself just a bit—without feeling guilty—if you are going to be a whole, integrated person. Loving other people as you love yourself means providing ample time for rest, recreation, and relaxation.

When your life is in balance you can expect:

Contentment

The Christian life is the only way of life that promises—and delivers—real, lasting contentment. For to be content, after all, means that you lack nothing. Every aspect of your life is in the proper balance. When Christ lives in you, you don't need anything else.

Contentment includes:

Peace:
Peace I bequeath to you; My peace I give to you. John 14:27
Thou wilt keep him in perfect peace, whose mind is stayed on thee: because he trusteth in thee. Isaiah 26:3 KJV
Satisfaction:
And the Lord shall guide thee continually, and satisfy thy soul in drought, and make fat thy bones: and thou shalt be like a watered garden, and like a spring of water, whose waters fail not. Isaiah 58:11 KJV
Lack of want:
. . . but those who seek the Lord shall lack in nothing good. Psalms 34:10. (Notice that we will not lack any *good* thing. Are all the things you want really good for you?)
Joy:
So may God, the fountain of hope, fill you with all joy and peace in your believing, so that you may enjoy overflowing hope by the power of the Holy Spirit. Romans 15:13
Thou hast . . . girded me with gladness, So that my soul may sing praise to Thee and not be silent. O Lord, my God, I will praise Thee forever. Psalms 30:11, 12

There is one prerequisite for contentment, however, and that is that your will must be aligned to His. If God's will for you is one thing and you want something else, your life will certainly be off-balance. But when you can honestly say, "Your will be done, Lord," all of life will fall into place in ways you never dreamed it could. Because He is in control and He has only your very best interests at heart.

*There are three things
which are too wonderful for me,
yes,
four which I do not comprehend:
the way of an eagle in the sky,
the way of a serpent upon a rock,
the way of a ship in the midst of
    the sea,
and
the way of a man with a maiden.*
                                Proverbs 30:18, 19

15

Intertwined

Looking Forward to Marriage

Many of you reading this book will one day marry. For you the
single years will be a transition period between adolescence and
marriage to the man of God's choice. If it seems like a long time
between adolescence and the altar, let me suggest a few reasons
why God may be allowing you to remain single for so long.

It goes without saying, perhaps, that marriage is for mature
people. And maturity and age usually go together. For that
reason, if for no other, waiting several years for marriage can be a
definite plus factor. The more mature you are, the easier your
adjustment to marriage will be. Perhaps at twenty or twenty-five
you weren't really mature enough for marriage (although you
may have thought you were). And even if you were mature,
perhaps your mate-to-be still had some growing up to do.

God knows exactly when (and if) you should marry and also
the person you are to marry. When it is the *right time* for you to

marry, He will bring you together. If you try to rush things you may end up marrying the wrong person with nothing ahead of you but years of heartache.

"God is never in a hurry, but He's always on time," someone once wrote. That statement was never more true than when it is applied to marriage. I was firmly convinced I was ready for marriage from the time I first discovered boys at age five. But God's timing required me to wait until I was thirty-two. When my husband and I finally met we soon discovered how important God's timing was in our lives. Through the years we had both changed and matured in areas that eventually brought us together. Had we met five or ten years earlier, chances are we wouldn't have given each other the time of day. But when in God's timing our paths finally crossed, we were ready for each other.

Are you really ready for marriage? Now is the time to get to know yourself—your strengths, your weaknesses, your assets, your liabilities. Just how mature are you? Are there areas where you still need to grow up? The better you understand yourself, the better able you will be to understand someone else.

Have you ever asked yourself *why* you want to get married? Yes, I *know* the desire to mate is inborn. But beyond the need for companionship and the desire to bear children, some women seek marriage for a variety of other reasons.

Some women want financial security. Is it the man—or his bank account—that sweeps you off your feet? (If at all possible, pay off all your bills before you get married. You'll feel good knowing your marriage was not motivated by a desperate attempt to get out of debt.)

Perhaps the desire to bear children is your primary motive. What happens then? Will your husband become simply a means to an end? A wise wife puts her husband *first* in her life (second only to Christ).

Some women marry to get away from their parents or to escape from loneliness. Take a good hard look at your motivation for marriage. The desire for companionship, children, and a legitimate outlet for your sexual needs is natural and normal. But there is a higher reason for marriage that should supercede all others. *Are you willing to choose marriage only if God shows you that that is the way in which you can serve Him best?*

Let's suppose now that you've found the one and only man (or think you have). The best way to insure a successful marriage is to carefully evaluate your relationship *before* you tie the knot.

Are You Both Committed Christians?

"No, but I'm working on him," you say. "He's never been interested in the church before, but he's really come around in the last few months since I've been witnessing to him."

Sorry to burst your bubble, but—you are probably headed for a lot of heartache. I am a firm believer that men should witness to men and women to women. I fully realize that there are exceptions to every rule. Occasionally God does use a woman to win her potential mate to Christ (or a man to win a woman). But in my experience those situations are rare. Why? Because there is an innate danger in a woman trying to win a man to her way of thinking.

If he really cares about you, he wants to be around you. And he knows that if he agrees to listen to you talk about your faith, it's a good way to spend time with you. And you, in turn, may be fooled by his pretended interest. He may even make a profession of faith in order to win your hand, although down deep inside he doesn't really mean it. And as the years unfold you discover that, spiritually speaking, you have little or nothing in common after all. I'm not saying that a man is necessarily deliberately deceitful. He may be. Or he may simply be fooling himself as well as you because his heart is so heavily involved.

It is too easy for emotions to overrule when members of the opposite sex try to win each other to Christ. I'm not saying you shouldn't share your faith with him. Of course you should. But if your boyfriend expresses an interest in knowing Christ personally, encourage him to talk it over with your minister or another Christian man. Then give him ample time to prove himself and mature in his newfound faith.

But suppose you both are already Christians. The most important element in marriage is your commitment to Christ and your desire to let Him control your marriage. Do you have a time of prayer and Bible study together? Have you both reached about the same level of maturity in your Christian faith? Is your husband-to-be a brand-new Christian? If he is very new to the faith, you might do well to delay marriage awhile until he has a chance to grow and mature in his faith. Otherwise he may feel spiritually inferior to you, which could cause problems later on.

Are your doctrinal beliefs similar? It certainly is not essential that you come from identical religious backgrounds, but beliefs that are extremely different can cause trouble later on. Married life is full of unexpected problems and crises that you can never predict in advance. During times of stress your beliefs can help bind you together — or separate you.

Ten weeks ago our first child was stillborn. Needless to say, it was a great shock and a disappointment to my husband and me. It never occurred to us when I went to the hospital that we would return home with empty arms.

During the weeks that have followed the death of our little one, my husband has been a great comfort to me. We are confident that our son is in God's care. But suppose our beliefs about life after death were extremely different. Suppose I believed our son is in heaven and George believed the child has been denied heaven because he was never baptized. My grief would have been twice as great. Or suppose I didn't believe there was life after death at all. What comfort could I be to him? Our comfort lies in the mutual assurance that our little boy is in God's loving care.

No two people will ever agree on everything doctrinally. But the closer you can come, the easier married life will be.

Sometimes minor differences can help to strengthen your beliefs. Suppose your financé thinks sprinkling is sufficient for baptism, but you are an immersionist all the way. Can you honestly prove from Scripture, beyond a shadow of a doubt, that immersion is the only mode of baptism God accepts? Can your fiancé prove that sprinkling is sufficient? Which is the most important, the mode of baptism or the desire of the heart in the one being baptized?

Evaluate your beliefs carefully and determine those things which are essential to the Christian faith—salvation by faith, God's ability to completely change our lives, the Resurrection, etc.—and stick to them. Don't let the minor points become points of contention in your marriage.

Do You Like Him?

You've already decided you love him, but liking a person is something else. You can love a person without liking him and you can like a person without being "in love" with him. In marriage it is essential that you like your husband as well as love him. Do you really enjoy being together and doing things together? Are your interests similar? Is he your *very best friend?* Are you *his* very best friend? If you can't honestly say you like each other, then why do you want to get married? (We're back to motives again.) Marriage is "till death do you part" and that will probably be a very long time. If you really enjoy each other's company, you can look forward to a wonderful lifetime together.

Do You Love Him for What He Is, or for What You Want Him to Become?

Once love-struck, it is easy to imagine a man to be something he isn't at all. Do you picture him conducting family prayers after you are married—when he refuses to pray with you now? Do you imagine him miraculously abandoning his violent temper after the wedding? Or playing happily with your children in the years to come, when he can hardly stand his nieces and nephews for five minutes now? This is a tough question, but one you must ask yourself if you want to be truly honest: *Would I really enjoy living with this man for the rest of my life if he never ever changed?*

Some women seem to have the idea that God has called them to change the world single-handedly—beginning with their husbands. And from the moment they say "I do," Operation

Transformation begins. They nag, scold, cry, beg, "tactfully" suggest, and maneuver to make their husbands become what they think he ought to be.

The woman who enters marriage planning to change her man is in for serious trouble. No man wants to be overhauled by his wife. Be honest with yourself. Do you want him to try and overhaul you? Do you want him to nag because you didn't do the dishes as soon as he thought you should, scold because you like to play tennis and he thinks bicycling would be better for your figure, or pretend to be jealous so you will do what he wants you to do when he wants you to do it?

When a woman tries to remake her husband, she is saying in essence, "I'm better than you. I licked that problem years ago. I would never do that. If you'd do it my way everything would be fine." And if that doesn't smack of self-righteousness I don't know what does. No matter how serious his fault, combating it with a self-righteous attitude makes two evils instead of only one.

The woman who nags and scolds destroys something beautiful in her marriage. By her actions she is saying to her husband, "I don't really like you. I wish you were different." How would you feel if your husband said that to you? Chances are you would ruffle your feathers in defense and determine never to change, so help you, Hannah.

If a man has a serious fault, the best way to help him change is to pray about the problem and keep your mouth shut. As you pray you may discover that *you* are the one who needs to change, not your husband. If his problem is something that needs to be discussed, God will show you the time and the place. Discuss it. Then drop the matter. Give each other the freedom to be yourselves — with all your good points and all your faults. A good marriage should result in growth and maturity — and it will if you both give each other the freedom to be yourselves.

How Does He Get Along With Other People?

How do other people react to him — his parents, brothers and sisters, friends, the people with whom he works? Does he have close friends as well as acquaintances? See each other in a variety of situations. Do people like him? Is he able to accept and enjoy most of the people he meets? Or does he tend to retreat from people or continually criticize them?

How Does He Treat You?

How does he treat you when you are around other people? Does he treat you with respect? Listen to your ideas? Encourage you to meet people and make friends? Or does he continually put you down in front of other people? Or become jealous if you talk to other men?

How do you treat him? Do you discuss his faults with other people? Embarrassing a man in public by talking about his bad points is a good way to drive him away. Are you loyal to each other?

Are You Honest With Each Other?

The most important question our minister asked us before we got married was, "Do you trust each other?" You can't answer that question truthfully until you honestly face your partner-to-be as he is. Since our marriage, I have not discovered anything of basic importance about my husband that I did not know before we got married. Because he is basically an honest person. He tells me what he thinks and feels and he accepts other people as is. When I hear stories of marriage breakups because the wife found out the husband was an alcoholic, or ran around with other women, or couldn't hold a job, I wonder why she never knew that before they got married. Obviously, somebody wasn't being honest.

Do You Think That Marriage Will Solve All Your Problems?

Come on, now, be honest. When two mature people get together, a beautiful relationship can be the result. When two immature people get together, it can only mean one thing — double trouble. Because of the intimacy of the marriage relationship, unresolved problems before marriage will probably intensify after marriage. If marriage to you is an escape hatch from the problems of life, you aren't ready to tie the knot.

Are You Mature Enough to Face the Fact That Love and Marriage Are High-Risk Commodities?

Can you commit your loved one to God—no matter what happens in the future?

In her book *In the Arena,* the late Isobel Kuhn, that great woman missionary to China, tells of a valuable lesson learned in this regard.

> The difficult lessons of 1942 taught me to *fear* leaning heavily on human props. I had surrendered husband, child, friends, all I possessed, long ago. But this was something deeper. This was relinquishing *my rights* to them. This was holding them, but on the open palm of my hand. (Mrs. McFarlane, principal of our language school in Yangchow and a dear warrior saint, had taught me that metaphor. She said, "Keep your treasures on the *open* palm of your hand. If you hold something tight clenched in your fist, God may have to hurt you in order to open your fingers and take it from you. But if it is offered on the *open palm* of your hand, you will hardly know when it is gone." I never found it so easy that I did not feel when my treasures were taken, but it did make a tremendous difference. It prevented me from collapsing or sprawling.)

Are You a Manipulator?

Both men and women manipulate people at one time or another. But women, I think, have a special proclivity for manipulation. I imagine it's because we're supposed to be the submissive members of society. And so rather than submit, we invent devious means to accomplish our desires without appearing aggressive. A woman who continually manipulates her husband and her marriage, however, is headed for trouble.

Everett Shostrom in his book *Man, the Manipulator,* suggests four kinds of manipulators. First there is the *active* manipulator —the aggressive person who takes advantage of other people's feelings of powerlessness and pushes them around. Then there is the *passive* manipulator. "Whereas the active manipulator wins by winning, the passive manipulator, paradoxically, wins by losing." He pretends to be helpless and stupid and lets the active manipulator do his thinking for him. The *competitive* manipulator views life as a battle and other people as competitors or enemies. His manipulation may be either active or passive, whatever the situation warrants. The fourth type is that of *indifferent manipulation.* "The manipulator plays hopeless, indifferent to, and withdraws from his contact with another. His stock phrase is 'I don't care.' . . . His methods are also both active and passive, sometimes playing the Nagger, Bitch, or Martyr, or Helpless."

Manipulation is an attempt to control another person, to make him see things your way, or do what you want him to do. The opposite of manipulation is freedom and openness. Freedom to let the other person be himself. And openness to discuss opinions and ideas, to listen to the other person's point of view. Do you and your fiancé discuss things openly? Or does one or the other of you always seem to get his way?

A false concept of what it means to be submissive has, I'm sure, led many a woman to develop manipulative techniques in order to get her way. Being submissive does not mean being a doormat for your husband to walk over—always giving in to him, always letting him have his own way. If your husband is mature, he doesn't want that kind of a relationship any more than you do.

Being submissive simply means that in any relationship somebody has to be the boss. Somebody has to make the final decision. If your husband wants to invest half of your savings in a gold mine and you want to keep all of it in the bank, obviously you can't do both. Somebody has to have the final say or you'll end up arguing until doomsday. Since God ordained that man is to be the head of the home, a submissive wife lets her husband make the final decision. Discuss the issue together. He wants your ideas as much as you want to express them. Chances are most of the time you will come to a decision that makes both of you happy. But in the event that he still feels his idea is best, give him the freedom (without any "I told you sos" if things don't work out) to do his own thing. The satisfaction of knowing that your husband is in charge is a valuable asset in any marriage.

Inherent in true submission is *trust*. Do you trust your fiancé's ability to take care of you? Then let him know you trust him by letting him make the final decision. A marriage that is based on mutual trust will deepen as the years go by.

There are many manipulative wives in this world who actively or passively control their husbands. And, unfortunately, many husbands let their wives get away with it. But I honestly don't believe that any normal woman deep down inside wants to control her husband.

Have You Had Premarital Counseling?

I strongly recommend premarital counseling for every engaged couple. No matter what kind of a job you hold, training and preparation are required. Yet most people seem to think they can jump into marriage with no preparation at all. How many divorces could have been prevented if the couple had known what they were getting into before they tied the knot?

Begin with the minister who will marry you. Discuss with him the duties and responsibilities of a Christian husband and wife—to each other, to other people, and to the children which will follow. Talk over problem areas and areas you think might become problems. It takes *three* people to establish a Christian home. Your minister will help you discover how to make *Christ* the head of your home.

In addition to your minister (if he is not trained in this area), a qualified counselor can provide counseling that will supplement that provided by your minister. Contact a psychiatrist, psychologist, licensed marriage counselor, or some other person who is qualified to administer tests designed to prepare you for marriage. These tests will help you better understand yourself and your fiancé and will pinpoint potential problem areas of which you may be completely unaware.

Two tests that should be basic to any counseling session are

the Taylor-Johnson Temperament Analysis and the Minnesota
Multiphasic Personality Inventory (MMPI).

Both you and your fiancé will take the Taylor-Johnson Temperament Analysis test, answering the questions according to the
way you see yourselves. Your scores will be charted on a graph
showing nine personality traits and their opposites:

nervous	composed
depressive	lighthearted
active-social	quiet
expressive-responsive	inhibited
sympathetic	indifferent
subjective	objective
dominant	submissive
hostile	tolerant
self-disciplined	impulsive

After you have completed the test, ask to take it again. This
time answer the questions according to the way you see your
fiancé, and he will answer according to the way he sees you.

For example, the first question on the test says, "Is _____ by
nature a forgiving person?" The first time you take the test you
place your own name in the blank space after "Is" and answer
accordingly. The second time around you insert the name of your
fiancé. The way you each perceive yourself may be quite different from the way you perceive each other. You may consider
yourself a very sympathetic person. Your fiancé may think you
are cold and indifferent. He may think he is quite aggressive. You
may see him as rather submissive.

Look at the profile sheet below left. The solid line shows how a
wife sees herself. The broken line superimposed over the solid
line shows how her husband sees her. Notice the similarities
(e.g., active-social) and the differences (e.g., indifferent, impulsive). Now look at the profile sheet on the right. The solid line
shows how the husband views himself. The broken line shows
how his wife sees him. Again notice the similarities and differences. Scores in the white area indicate that further counseling is

TAYLOR-JOHNSON TEMPERAMENT ANALYSIS PROFILE
Profile Revision of 1967

These Answers Describe **BROWN, RICHARD**   Age **46**   Sex **M**   Date **8-1-66**

School **U of CALIF.**   Grade_____ Degree **Ph.D.** Major **CHEM. ENG.** Occupation **CHEM·ENGINEER**   Counselor **W.E.**

Single____ Years Married **20** Years Divorced____ Years Widowed____ Children: M **1** Ages **18**   F **1** Ages **16**

Answers made by: SELF (circled) husband, wife, father, mother, son, daughter, brother, sister, or_____ of the person described.

Norm(s):'67-'68 G.P. c.c.	A		B		C		D		E		F		G		H		I		Attitude (Sten) Score: **6 6**
Mids	**4**	**1**	**2**	**2**	**2**	**1**			**1**	**1**	**1**		**2**			**1**	**1**		Total Mids: **6 13**
Raw score	**4**	**10**	**7**	**8**	**20**	**12**	**17**	**6**	**34**	**19**	**1**	**9**	**20**	**10**	**8**	**2**	**37**	**37**	Raw score
Percentile	**20**	**36**	**50**	**39**	**19**	**13**	**11**	**2**	**65**	**23**	**5**	**36**	**26**	**9**	**39**	**9**	**96**	**95**	Percentile
TRAIT	Nervous		Depressive		Active-Social		Expressive-Responsive		Sympathetic		Subjective		Dominant		Hostile		Self-disciplined		TRAIT

TRAIT OPPOSITE	Composed	Light-hearted	Quiet	Inhibited	Indifferent	Objective	Submissive	Tolerant	Impulsive	TRAIT OPPOSITE

Graph with vertical scale from 5 to 95

■ Excellent   ■ Acceptable   ▨ Improvement desirable   □ Improvement urgent

DEFINITIONS

TRAITS

Nervous — Tense, high-strung, apprehensive.
Depressive — Pessimistic, discouraged, dejected.
Active-Social — Energetic, enthusiastic, socially involved.
Expressive-Responsive — Spontaneous, affectionate, demonstrative.
Sympathetic — Kind, understanding, compassionate.
Subjective — Emotional, illogical, self-absorbed.
Dominant — Confident, assertive, competitive.
Hostile — Critical, argumentative, punitive.
Self-disciplined — Controlled, methodical, persevering.

OPPOSITES

Composed — Calm, relaxed, tranquil.
Light-hearted — Happy, cheerful, optimistic.
Quiet — Socially inactive, lethargic, withdrawn.
Inhibited — Restrained, unresponsive, repressed.
Indifferent — Unsympathetic, insensitive, unfeeling.
Objective — Fair-minded, reasonable, logical.
Submissive — Passive, compliant, dependent.
Tolerant — Accepting, patient, humane.
Impulsive — Uncontrolled, disorganized, changeable.

Note: Important decisions should not be made on the basis of this profile without confirmation of these results by other means.

Reproduced by permission of Psychological Publications, Inc. *Taylor-Johnson Temperament Analysis* (T-JTA), Taylor, Robert M. and Morrison, Lucile Phillips, by Psychological Publications, Inc., 5300 Hollywood Blvd., Los

CRISS - CROSS

TAYLOR-JOHNSON TEMPERAMENT ANALYSIS PROFILE
Profile Revision of 1967

These Answers Describe **BROWN, HELEN** _____ Age **40** Sex **F** Date **8-1-66**

School **COMPLETED** Grade **11** Degree _____ Major _____ Occupation **HOUSEWIFE** _____ Counselor **W.E.**

Single _____ Years Married **20** Years Divorced _____ Years Widowed _____ Children: M **1** Ages **18** F **1** Ages **16**

Answers made by: SELF **and** husband, wife, father, mother, son, daughter, brother, sister, or _____ of the person described.

Norm(s): 67-68 G.P. C.C.	A		B		C		D		E		F		G		H		I		Attitude (Step) Score: 5 4
Mids		2	1		1		3	1	5	1	4	2		1	1	1	4	1	Total Mids: 19 9
Raw score	16	28	18	21	36	37	37	33	35	19	20	24	32	33	13	25	18	29	Raw score
Percentile	66	90	72	74	94	94	87	72	60	23	81	84	96	89	71	80	23	68	Percentile
TRAIT	Nervous		Depressive		Active-Social		Expressive-Responsive		Sympathetic		Subjective		Dominant		Hostile		Self-disciplined		TRAIT

| TRAIT OPPOSITE | Composed | Light-hearted | Quiet | Inhibited | Indifferent | Objective | Submissive | Tolerant | Impulsive | TRAIT OPPOSITE |

Excellent   Acceptable   Improvement desirable   Improvement urgent

DEFINITIONS

TRAITS

Nervous — Tense, high-strung, apprehensive.
Depressive — Pessimistic, discouraged, dejected.
Active-Social — Energetic, enthusiastic, socially involved.
Expressive-Responsive — Spontaneous, affectionate, demonstrative.
Sympathetic — Kind, understanding, compassionate.
Subjective — Emotional, illogical, self-absorbed.
Dominant — Confident, assertive, competitive.
Hostile — Critical, argumentative, punitive.
Self-disciplined — Controlled, methodical, persevering.

OPPOSITES

Composed — Calm, relaxed, tranquil.
Light-hearted — Happy, cheerful, optimistic.
Quiet — Socially inactive, lethargic, withdrawn.
Inhibited — Restrained, unresponsive, repressed.
Indifferent — Unsympathetic, insensitive, unfeeling.
Objective — Fair-minded, reasonable, logical.
Submissive — Passive, compliant, dependent.
Tolerant — Accepting, patient, humane.
Impulsive — Uncontrolled, disorganized, changeable.

Note: Important decisions should not be made on the basis of this profile without confirmation of these results by other means.

Angeles, CA 90027, 1966–1973. The two T-JTA profiles depicted above represent only a portion of a complete T-JTA marital testing.

vitally necessary. Scores in the black area indicate that all is well. Scores in the other two shaded areas indicate that the person's profile is acceptable (dark area) or improvement is desirable (light area).

The value of this test is that it can give you new insights into yourselves and each other and the way you think and feel.

The second test, the Minnesota Multiphasic Personality Inventory (MMPI), is designed to objectively evaluate your personality and pinpoint major psychological problems — such as psychopathic deviations, paranoia, schizophrenia, etc. You may be thoroughly convinced that neither of you has any serious psychological problems, but it never hurts to make sure. If you discover from the test that there is a problem, you have the advantage of being able to deal with it before you get married. If you discover that neither of you has any serious problems, it is a good feeling to know that before you enter marriage.

Your counselor may wish to administer any of several other good tests. But these two (or ones similar) are especially helpful. Ask your minister and your counselor to recommend books you can read together to further prepare you for marriage. Any device that can help you discover and discuss potential problems in your marriage before you get married is time well-spent and money well-invested. Be careful, however, that you do not use the knowledge of each other's problem areas as clubs. ("It's just like the counselor said. You are *so* stubborn.") Pray about the trouble spots and work together to overcome them. Some can be resolved rather quickly, others may require further counseling.

Like many other aspects of living, premarital counseling involves risk — and it costs money. Are you willing to discover things about yourself and your partner (both good and bad) that you didn't know before? Are you willing to face the possibility that premarital counseling *might* reveal that you two are not at all suitable for each other?

If your fiancé refuses to have premarital counseling, you had better reconsider your marriage plans. What if some serious problems arose after your marriage? If he won't accept counseling now, don't expect him to seek help later on. Premarital counseling is one way God may use to confirm to you both that marriage to each other is, or is not, His will.

The Final Test

The final test of whether or not you are ready for marriage is this: *Are you both willing to grow and change?* None of us is perfect and nobody that I know of has ever had a prefect marriage. But a truly successful marriage—and there are many of them—is successful because both partners are willing to grow and change. Neither partner thinks that he is always right. Both are open to new ideas and new ways of doing things.

The Christian life, whether you are married or single, is a series of changes that produce that all-important growth. Jesus said, "I have come so they may have life and have it abundantly." There can be no life without growth. And growth involves making mistakes, saying "I'm sorry" (to God and to your partner), and starting over again. As Audrey Lee Sands puts it in her book *Single & Satisfied:*

> There is no better preparation for commitment to a husband than commitment to Christ. If you know what it means to obey your Lord out of love and devotion, it won't be difficult to be submissive to your husband. If you have become one with Christ in heart and mind, it won't be hard for you to identify with a life companion. If you have sought to understand and to delight in the will of your Heavenly Father, then you will have a minimum of marital adjustment problems. The more perfectly you love the Lord, the more perfect will be your marriage relationship. It was not by chance that the Holy Spirit chose the marriage relationship to symbolize Christ's relationship to the Church.

Whether you find fulfillment in the single life or in marriage, I pray that you will have the abundant life God has promised. It's free for the taking. Reach out to Him and He will guide you through every moment of your life ahead.

DATE DUE